Eschatology:

End-Time Views Compared

By

Dr. Cecil Sanders

FWB
Publications

Copyright 2017 by Cecil Sanders
ISBN 978-1-940609-25-6 Soft cover
All scripture verses are from the KJV Translations
This book was printed in the United States of America.

To order additional copies of this book, contact:
Dr. Cecil Sanders, 14570 HWY 189, New Edinburg, Arkansas 71660
Or www.amazon.com

Columbus, Ohio

Contents

Preface

Much of the human race has an innate curiosity about the future. This curiosity is greatly heightened by a number of writers and television personalities who over speculate on the meaning of Bible prophecies. Prophecy is important to the hope of Christians and therefore should be rightly understood. However, rightly understanding that which is interpreted so many different ways is not always an easy task. Much of the confusion is caused by a hyperliteral method of interpreting Bible prophecy that is found in apocalyptic sections such as Daniel and Revelation. This method of interpretation, when contrasted with others, is sometimes incorrectly and even arrogantly presented. If one accepts it, he is seen as a Bible believer; if not, he is considered a non-Bible believer. Literalism is equated with orthodoxy. It will be necessary, therefore, to deal with hermeneutics in an early part of this work.

The purpose of this book is not intended to create controversy, although it is critical of what is considered serious errors in dispensationalism. In the interest of Christian harmony, the temptation is to remain silent. Silence, however, does not promote the communication of truth.

The views expressed in this book are strictly personal. There is no attempt to speak for the denomination to which the author belongs or for denominational institutions, one from which he has graduated and another where he taught for 15 years. These can speak for themselves. The author presents what he believes to be correct interpretations of prophecy with firm enough conviction and language to justify their acceptance. It will be verified that conservative or evangelical believers do not have to be dispensationalists; there are other options.

A second expressed purpose of this book is to clarify the various views of eschatology, a study of the last things. Hopefully the reader will not only be able to determine if he/she is a premillennialist, a postmillennialist, or an amillennialist but will also be able to determine his/her particular type of premillennialism, postmillennialism, or amillennialism. Within each of these systems of interpretation there are options open to the reader; the options however are limited. One may disagree on several points and still be a premillennialist, but there are certain basics that must be accepted. This is also true in the postmillennial and amillennial systems.

A third purpose is to establish from the Bible a clear arrangement of God's plans for the future without erroneous, confusing, or speculative theorizing.

A fourth purpose is to create an awareness of the importance of eschatology. The world dare not take lightly what God's Word has placed so much emphasis upon. Eschatology is much more than curiosity about the future; it has much to do with one's attitude concerning Arabic and Israeli disputes. If the people of a nation believe Israel remains God's chosen people, then they may blindly support Israel without any consideration of justice. That can cause hatred, murder, and even war.

This book is presented with a prayer that it will be a blessing to both its readers and the world at large. There is no attempt to prove the Bible; the Scriptures are herein accepted as truth. While reading this book, one should search the Scriptures to obtain tools for the present and truth concerning the future. The reader may look forward to an orderly presentation of eschatology in which alternative views are compared. The first purpose for anyone studying prophecy and eschatology is to build his/her understanding of God's future plans. No person can share with others what he/she does not have.

Cecil Sanders

Chapter 1

Prophecy and Millennial Views

Broadly speaking there are three general millennial systems of thought, each professing to set forth true Biblical eschatology – a study of events that were future at the time they were predicted. These systems of thought are premillennialism, postmillennialism, and amillennialism. In addition to these three broad views, there are distinct variations within each system which can be of major significance.

In spite of differences, there are also important similarities which the various millennial systems should hold in common. These similarities are:

1. That each system can and does accept all Scriptures as the inspired Word of God; that is, each professes to be based upon Biblical teachings.

2. That each recognizes there will be a future, visible, and bodily return of Christ.

3. That each accepts the divinity of Christ and believes in His substitutionary atonement.

4. That each holds that every individual will at some time receive a resurrected body which will live eternally either in Heaven or Hell.

5. That differences in belief result from different methods of interpretation rather than from a lack of loyalty to the Bible.

6. That each system of interpretation is held by able conservative and evangelical scholars.

Broad definitions for each of the millennial views with variations are as follows:

Premillennialism in General

All schools of premillennialism generally hold the following concepts:

1. That the world is growing worse and will continue to do so until Christ comes and personally establishes His kingdom on earth.

2. That Christ will establish a kingdom which was promised by Old Testament prophets and not fulfilled during His first advent.

3. That a personal, visible, and earthly reign of Christ will precede, by at least a thousand years, the end of the world by fire.

4. That we are near the end of the church age, and the return of Christ could occur within the lifetime of this generation.

5. That before and during a future tribulation period, the Jews will be restored to the land of Israel.

6. That the two resurrections alluded to in Revelation 20:1-10 are both bodily resurrections.

7. That when Christ returns, the righteous dead will be resurrected in what is called the first resurrection. There

is no agreement, however, on when this will happen or if the rapture will include all the righteous dead.

8. That the resurrected righteous and the living transformed righteous will together be raptured to meet Christ in the air. Some premillennialists place this event before the expected tribulation, some in the middle of it, and others following it.

9. That a judgment of the righteous will follow the rapture.

10. That Christ at His return will destroy the man of sin, beast, or antichrist in the Battle of Armageddon.

11. That when Christ comes there will be a National Conversion of Israel.

12. That a Judgment of Nations will precede the millennium (Matt. 25:31-46).

13. That following the victory at Armageddon and the Judgment of Nations, Christ will establish His kingdom with Jerusalem as its capital.

14. That at the beginning of the millennium, Satan will be bound and placed in the abyss.

15. That Christ will rule the whole world for a thousand years in righteousness, peace, and prosperity. The thousand years, however, is sometimes not taken to be exact, but is believed to represent an extended period of time.

16. That the curse upon nature will be removed, causing the land to become very productive. Ferocious animals will be changed so as to live in peace with themselves and with mankind. Human life will be prolonged but death and sickness will not be totally banished.

17. That those born during the millennium and not converted, will be held in control by Christ.

18. That near the end of the millennium Satan will be loosed for a "little season" and will deceive many nations into making war against the saints. This battle will be known as the Battle of Gog and Magog.

19. That at Gog and Magog, Christ will defeat Satan and soon thereafter cast him into the lake of fire for eternity.

20. That about this time the wicked dead will be resurrected. After being judged in the Great White Throne Judgment, they also will be cast into the lake of fire for eternity.

21. That the final state of the redeemed will be ushered in immediately after the Great White Throne Judgment (Rev. 20:11-15).

Historical Premillennialism

Historical or classical premillennialism, originally called chiliasm, is the oldest and mildest form of premillennialism. It has several distinctive characteristics in addition to the general beliefs of premillennialism. They are as follows:

1. It is characterized by a futuristic method of interpretation; yet, it is significantly different from the dispensational variety.

2. It does not emphasize an any-moment return of Christ. Its advocates hold that a number of events must happen before Christ returns. Discernible signs include the worldwide proclamation of a single antichrist different from all other antichrists and a Great Tribulation period.

3. It holds that there is only one future coming of Christ and that it will follow, not precede, the tribulation

period. This coming is one-stage and visible. It will be accompanied by the first resurrection and rapture after which believers will almost immediately escort Christ back to earth.

4. It holds, in contrast to dispensationalists, that Israel, saved and restored, is not to be considered a separate people since there is only one people of God – the body of Christ. It places no emphasis upon God having a separate purpose for Israel and the church, the first being earthly and the second heavenly. The gospel proclaimed by Jews during the tribulation is the gospel of grace, not a separate gospel of the kingdom. The church has replaced national Israel as God's elect.

5. It holds that the church will be on earth during the tribulation period.

6. It holds to a less literal approach to eschatology than its dispensational counterpart. Historical premillennialists are often unsure concerning the length of the tribulation period, the length of the millennium, and a detailed program of fulfilled Old Testament prophecy during the millennium.

There are also several variations within historical premillennialism. A few hold that the millennial kingdom is primarily Jewish in nature, but some allow Gentile believers a subordinate place. Others hold that it is the martyrs, Jewish or otherwise, who will occupy the primary place. Some hold that during the millennium all those with physical bodies will be subject to death; others say only unbelievers will be subject to death.

Historical premillennialists are either vague or silent concerning the relationship of those with spiritual bodies living in the presence of those with physical bodies, including some who remain unconverted. They are also vague on the subject and place of the restored temple with its animal sacrifices. Perhaps it is because many writers feel it is best to say as little as possible about subjects on which there is no clear revelation. In many ways these premillennialists are more like amillennialists than they are their fellow dispensationalists.

Dispensational Premillennialism

Dispensationalism is considered by all non-dispensationalists as a system of interpretation not born until the 19th century. They also consider dispensationalism to be radical in nature. Dispensationalists, however, conceive of their beliefs either as a needed refinement of historical premillennialism or as rediscovered truth. They differ so greatly from other premillennialists that writers often list them as a separate system rather than as an alternate form of premillennialism. The distinctive beliefs of dispensationalists include the following:

1. That the Bible must be interpreted literally where possible, including apocalyptic, poetic, and prophetic literature. The historical and prophetical parts of the Bible must be interpreted alike. All prophecy either has been or will be fulfilled literally. All Old Testament promises were made to physical Israel, never to spiritual Israel or the church, and must be fulfilled in physical Israel.

2. That a sharp distinction must be made between Israel and the church. God has an unconditional covenant with Israel through Abraham and regardless of obedience or disobedience, Israel remains forever the chosen people of God; they must experience every promise made to them. God's ultimate purpose for the church will be fulfilled in Heaven while His ultimate purpose for Israel will be fulfilled on the earth. Some hold that Jews and Gentiles will forever be separated with the Jewish believers living on the new

earth and the Gentile believers living in the new heavens. Any concept of the New Testament church replacing Old Testament Israel and of God fulfilling His promise to His Old Testament people through the church is rejected. Old Testament promises to Israel are not simply promises to God's people that can find fulfillment in New Testament believers; they are promises to fleshly Israel and can be fulfilled only in fleshly Israel.

3. That the church was totally unforeseen in Old Testament prophecy. The church resulted from the Jewish rejection of the kingdom offered to them and the subsequent crucifixion of Christ. The church is looked upon as a parenthesis in time. John F. Walvoord, a dispensationalist, commented: *"...The present age is a parenthesis or a time period not predicted by the Old Testament and therefore not fulfilling or advancing the program of events revealed in the Old Testament foreview."*[1]

God dealt with His people – the Jews – until they crucified their Messiah; His prophetic time-clock then stopped for the duration of the unpredicted church age. Sixty-nine weeks of Daniel's vision (Dan. 9:24-27) concerning the chosen people were fulfilled before they crucified their Messiah; God's clock stopped at that time. At the pretribulation rapture of the church, God's clock will start again. The clock stopped because the kingdom was postponed, and God's predicted program for Israel was interrupted. The clock will start again only when the church is out of the way and God returns to His program with Israel. The period which will follow the pretribulation rapture is believed to be Daniel's 70th week on the prophetic time-clock, and it is totally unrelated to the church.

4. That a distinction must be made between the "Kingdom of Heaven" and the "Kingdom of God." The Kingdom of Heaven is the kingdom that was offered to the

Dr. Cecil Sanders
Eschatology: End-Time Views Compared

Jews at Christ's first coming. It was Jewish or Messianic in nature; it, therefore, had to be postponed after it was rejected. On the other hand, the Kingdom of God is broad, inclusive, and universal in nature. It includes saved Jews and Gentiles of all ages; this form of the kingdom, therefore, is a present reality. This is the "mystery" or church form of the kingdom, but it is not to be identified with the kingdom so often predicted in the Old Testament.

5. That much of the New Testament is not applicable to the church age; it applies to a future kingdom age. Depending upon what dispensational material one is reading, all or part of the Gospels and almost all of Revelation are for the kingdom age. In the Gospels, it is often pointed out that the Sermon on the Mount and the Lord's Prayer apply only to the kingdom age which had to be postponed. Some say that the early epistles are kingdom age in nature and that the instructions to the Jewish church in Acts do not apply to the Gentile church.

6. That dispensationalists, in contrast with other premillennialists, zealously advocate the imminent or any-moment return of Christ.

7. That worship during the millennium will center around a rebuilt Jewish temple in the city of Jerusalem. Animal sacrifices will be reinstituted, but not necessarily as propitiatory offerings; some think of them as memorial in nature (Ezek. 40-48).

8. That there are from four to seven dispensations (innocence, conscience or freedom, human government, promise or pilgrim law, law or Israel, grace or church, and kingdom or manifestation); eight covenants (the Edenic covenant before the fall, a covenant after the fall with Adam, Noah, Abraham, Moses, David, the Palestinian covenant, and the new covenant by Christ); a two- or possibly three-

staged Second Coming (one before the tribulation period, one at the end of the tribulation, and one following the millennium to burn the present world); three or four resurrections (the righteous before the tribulation, the righteous who die during the millennium, and the wicked dead after the millennium); and from four to eight judgments (the judgment of saints following a pretribulation rapture, the judgment of Israel, the judgment of the living Gentile nations before the millennium, the judgment for the saints who die during the tribulation period and /or the millennium, the judgment of the believer's sins by Christ on the cross, and the believer's judgment of self).

9. That the Second Coming of Christ is not a single event, but it includes two and possibly three stages separated by over a thousand years. Stage one is the pretribulation rapture of the church and does not include Old Testament saints. Stage one concerns the church alone; Christ secretly raptures it away from tribulation. Stage or phase two follows the tribulation which is generally believed to be seven years in length and is to be identified with Daniel's seventieth week (Dan. 9:24-27). Stage two will concern Israel and the world when Christ comes *with* His church. Stage two is between the tribulation and the millennium. Stage three, necessitated by this system, will occur when Christ comes to burn the present world (2 Pet. 3). Chronologically this is after the millennium but before the creation of a new heaven and earth. Therefore, stage one precedes stage two by seven years, and stage two precedes stage three by approximately a thousand years (see chart).

10. That when Christ returns to secretly rapture the church, He will not descend to the earth but will be joined by the church in the air and will remain there during a seven-year earthly tribulation period. Christians will be judged at the Judgment Seat of Christ while in the air (2 Cor. 5:10, 11).

The Marriage Feast of the Lamb follows this judgment, and it is also in the air.

11. That during this seven-year absence of Christ and the church a number of events will occur on earth: (1) Daniel's predicted tribulation period begins (Dan. 9:24-27); (2) an antichrist reigns and during the last half of the reign, he severely punishes all those who fail to worship him as God; (3) terrible judgments fall upon the earth (Rev. 4-19); (4) a remnant of Israel numbering 144,000 will accept Christ as their Messiah (Rev. 7:3-8); (5) this remnant will begin preaching the "gospel of the kingdom"- the same kingdom that Christ had earlier proclaimed as being at hand but then had to postpone; (6) these Jewish evangelists, sometimes referred to as 144,000 Billy Grahams, will witness the conversion of an innumerable Gentile multitude (Rev. 7:9); and (7) the antichrist or beast along with the false prophet prepare their forces to attack the people of God in what will be known as the Battle of Armageddon.

12. That Christ will come *with* His saints at this point and defeat the opposing forces of evil in the Battle of Armageddon. About this time Christ will also witness the national conversion of Israel, a conversion much larger than the earlier tribulation remnant conversion.

13. That between His coming and the millennium, there will be a separate judgment of Israel (Ezek. 20:33-38). Living Jewish rebels will be put to death and denied the millennial experience; living Israelites who accept Christ will enter the millennial kingdom.

14. That between Christ's coming and the millennium, there will also be a judgment of living Gentile nations- the sheep and goat judgment (Matt. 25:31-46). Resurrected people will have no part in this judgment; living Gentiles will be judged according to how they have treated

God's people during the tribulation. The sheep will remain on earth and enter into the millennium; the goats will be cast into the lake of fire.

15. That between Christ's Second Coming and the millennium, a resurrection for the tribulation saints will occur. Since Old Testament saints were not included in the earlier resurrection of church saints, they will also rise (Rev. 20:4). These resurrected people, however, will not enter the millennial kingdom but will depart for the New Jerusalem in the sky.

16. That at the beginning of the millennium, which will last exactly a thousand years, Satan will be bound.

17. That the millennial kingdom, which will follow the binding of Satan, will be a fulfillment of Old Testament promises to Israel. Israelites will be exalted above Gentiles; however, no spirit of jealousy is anticipated. Dispensationalists usually exclude all resurrected believers, Jews or Gentiles, from the millennium. Charles C. Ryrie wrote:

The earthly purpose of Israel of which dispensationalists speak concerns the national promise which will be fulfilled by Jews during the millennium as they live on the earth in UNRESURRECTED bodies. The earthly future for Israel does not concern Israelites who die before the millennium is set up.[2]

18. That when the millennial kingdom is first set up it will consist of only earthly saved people. These people will marry, reproduce, and die. And although their offspring may rebel against Christ, the millennium will be a golden age far greater than anything the world has ever experienced.

19. That during the millennium, resurrected saints will live above the earth in the New Jerusalem; this city is

expected to later descend to a newly created earth (Rev. 21:20-22:5). These resurrected saints will, however, participate with Christ in certain judgments (Matt. 19:28; 1 Cor. 6:2; and Rev. 20:6). In a limited way they will alternate between the New Jerusalem and the earth. This seems to be the position of both J. Dwight Pentecost[3] and John F. Walvoord.[4]

20. That before the millennium is over, there will be another resurrection which will consist of all believers who die during the millennium.

21. That those born during the millennium who do not become true converts to Christ will, after Satan is loosed, be led to attack the "camp of the saints."

22. That following the millennium there will be another resurrection for all the unbelieving dead who will be judged at the Great White Throne Judgment (Rev. 20:11-15). Dispensationalists hold there will be no believers involved in this judgment.

23. That at this time the final state will be ushered in as the New Jerusalem and her people will descend to the new earth. Some hold that after the New Jerusalem descends, Jews and Gentiles will dwell together forever without losing their identity. Others hold that the final state for the Gentile believers will be in Heaven above; the final state for Jewish believers will be on an earth promised specifically to them.[5]Among dispensationalists, therefore, there is agreement that the status of the Jews will forever be distinct, but there is no agreement concerning a separate eternal dwelling place.

Pretribulation Premillennialism

The difference between pretribulation premillennialism and dispensational pretribulation premillennialism is relatively small. All dispensationalists are pretribulationists, but all pretribulationists are not dispensationalists. Most American pretribulationists, however, are dispensational. Contrary to dispensationalism, some pretribulationists teach a partial-rapture before the tribulation. Only those Christians who are watching and ready will be raptured after they are refined and made ready, that is, after experiencing the tribulation. Those of the partial-rapture persuasion are, therefore, pretribulationists but not totally so. They are also posttribulationists.

This alternate form of pretribulationism illustrates the possibility of variety in pretribulation premillennialism itself. There are disagreements on points other than the partial-rapture theory. The partial-rapture theory naturally leads to the concept that the church is not necessarily exempt from tribulation; this concept is, of course rejected by dispensationalists. There could also be disagreement concerning the separation of Israel and the church. Two recognized writers who believe in the partial-rapture theory are Robert G. Govett and George H. Lang.

Midtribulation Premillennialism

Midtribulation is a term that describes those who believe a rapture of the church will occur in the middle of a future seven-year tribulation period rather than at the beginning or at the end of it. The church will go through the first half of the Great Tribulation which is believed to be the first half of Daniel's seventieth week of prophecy. The term "Midtribulation" is not a good term for many of those who wear the label. What they really believe is that a rapture of the church will occur in the middle of Daniel's seventieth week of prophecy. To some so-called midtribulationists this is also the beginning of the Great Tribulation which will last three and a half rather than seven years. This belief in a three and a half rather than seven year tribulation period means these interpreters are actually pretribulationists rather than midtribulationists. Norman B. Harrison is an example of a midtribulationist improperly named.[6]

Others of this group seem to talk about a little tribulation during the first half of the period and much tribulation during the last half. This sounds like a seven-year tribulation period with the intensity changing at its midpoint. The church suffers a little from the wrath of man during the first half but escapes the wrath of God during the second half. The use of the word "Midtribulation" is appropriate for this type of language but inappropriate when applied to the whole group.

More important than the small difference concerning the time of the rapture is the difference midtribulationists and dispensationalists have on the issue of Israel and the church. Midtribulationists often teach that people converted after the rapture will still become part of the church because God has only one body, the body of Christ which is the church. Old Testament prophecies directed to Israel *as the people of God* can be fulfilled in the New Testament people of God, a racially mixed church. However, Old Testament prophecies directed to Israel *as a nation* must be fulfilled in national Israel. On the important issues of Israel and the church both midtribulationists and posttribulationists generally disagree with dispensationalists. For example, the "elect" spoken of in the Olivet Discourse (Matt. 24:22; Mk. 13:20) are not interpreted as Jews but as believers or church saints. Furthermore, the "fig tree" (Matt. 24:32-35) is not limited to natural Israel.[7]

Posttribulation Premillennialism

Almost all posttribulationists are historical premillennialists whose views have already been presented. In addition to historical premillennialism, there are two other varieties of posttribulationism.

First, those who believe in a partial-rapture are both pretribulationists and posttribulationists. Christians who are ready will be raptured before the tribulation, and Christians who are not ready will be raptured after the tribulation.

A second type of posttribulationist believes the Great Tribulation will take place during the first half of Daniel's seventieth week. The church will suffer greatly under the hand of a future antichrist. The last half of the week is a period of God's wrath and is not believed to be part of the Great Tribulation. Christ will come for the rapture of the church during the middle of Daniel's seventieth prophetic week; nevertheless, according to this view, His coming will be posttribulational. For a thorough discussion of this type of posttribulational premillennialism one may consider the work of John T. Sharrit.[8]

Amillennialists might even be considered a type of posttribulationism since they believe Christ will return after the tribulation is over. They are not, of course, a type of premillennial posttribulationism.

Postmillennialism

Postmillennialism is an eschatological view which holds that the Kingdom of God is slowly and presently being extended over the earth through the preaching of the gospel under the power of the Holy spirit, that the world will essentially be Christianized, and that Christ will return at the CLOSE of a long period of earthly peace and righteousness commonly called the millennium. Postmillennialists are not overly enthused about the word "millennium" since their concept of the millennium does not basically come from Revelation 20.

Specific expectations and concepts of post-millennialism include the following:

1. Postmillennialists expect that prophecy given in figurative or symbolic language may be fulfilled the same way. While premillennialists claim to hold to a rigid literal interpretation of Bible prophecy, postmillennialists accept a figurative or spiritual interpretation if the evidence indicates that it is preferable.

2. Postmillennialists expect the vast majority of the world to be converted before Christ returns. This will not simply be a human achievement; it will be a divine achievement accomplished by the successful proclamation of the gospel under the convicting power of the Holy Ghost. It is not claimed that every individual will be converted. Christian principles will, however, be the rule of society rather than the exception.

3. Postmillennialists consider the Kingdom of God primarily as a present reality on earth. It is not a domain over which Christ visibly rules; instead, it is Christ ruling in the hearts of people. The Kingdom of God is believed to have been in existence since the beginning of the world and was more clearly revealed at the first coming of Christ.

4. Postmillennialists expect the Kingdom of God to have gradual rather than sudden and dramatic growth. While premillennialists expect the kingdom to be suddenly and dramatically set up by Christ AFTER He returns, postmillennialists expect the kingdom to slowly grow as the gospel is spread throughout the world BEFORE Christ returns.

5. Postmillennialists expect a long period of earthly peace and righteousness, commonly called the millennium, before Christ returns. It is perhaps much longer than a literal thousand years. It is believed to be symbolic of an earthly golden age of indefinite length. Some hold the millennium covers the entire church age while others see the church age merge into the millennium in such a way that a beginning point is hardly discernable.

6. Postmillennialists do not expect an imminent or any-moment return of Christ. When opponents object to the postmillennial view of World Christianization on the basis of present world conditions, postmillennialists point out that there is yet plenty of time before Christ returns.

7. Postmillennialists do expect that there will be a flare-up of evil near the end of the millennium. Both premillennialists and postmillennialists have a problem with this prediction because it seems contradictory and out of place in both systems of thought. Both, at times, make attempts to give possible solutions. Both generally claim, however, that it is not their responsibility to explain why God allows this flare-up of sin; that is His business.

8. Postmillennialists interpret Daniel's 70 prophetic weeks as realized eschatology; that is, as fulfilled. There is no connection between end-time tribulation and Daniel's 70th week. The length of the end-time tribulation is, therefore, not likely to be seven years.

9. Postmillennialists expect a future conversion of Israel along with all nations. This is not a fulfillment of prophecy concerning National Israel as a separate people of God. Israel will simply be converted and become part of the church. It is not Israel as a nation that has a predicted future, but the Israel of God which is the church. This Israel of God consists of both Jews and Gentiles.

10. Postmillennialists expect the earthly millennium to end, not begin, with the personal, visible, and bodily return of Christ.

11. Postmillennialists expect a future single General Resurrection and General Judgment with the eternal state to follow shortly thereafter.

12. Postmillennialists generally interpret Revelation 20:1-6 exclusively as a martyr scene. These martyrs, seen earlier in Revelation 6, are in soul form in Heaven. They reign with Christ from Heaven while the millennium is taking place on earth. The first resurrection is spiritual and takes place when a soul is regenerated or born again. The second resurrection is bodily in nature and includes both the righteous and unrighteous dead. This second resurrection takes place immediately before the Great White Throne Judgment. Some postmillennialists, however, interpret the first resurrection as life in the intermediate state rather than as the regeneration of the soul. Also, these do not interpret Revelation 20:1-6 exclusively as a martyr scene. The activities described in Revelation 20:1-3 take place on earth while the activities described in Revelations 20:4-6 are related to the intermediate state.

Amillennialism

Amillennialism is an eschatological view which generally holds that the millennium of the Bible, found only in Revelation 20, is a heavenly scene. They think it is a reality only for righteous souls or disembodied spirits in the intermediate state. Some amillennialists, however, believe the millennium of Revelation 20 also includes the regenerate who have not yet died.

Specific expectations or concepts of amillennialism include the following:

1. Amillennialists, like postmillennialists, expect that prophecy given in figurative or symbolic language may be fulfilled in a non-literal way. They accept a figurative or spiritual interpretation if the evidence indicates that it is preferable.

2. Amillennialists expect good and evil to continue to exist side by side until Christ returns. Instead of the Bible predicting that the world will grow better, as postmillennialists teach, it is expected to grow worse according to amillennialists. This does not, however, lessen the responsibility of amillennialists to carry out the Great Commission of Christ.

3. Amillennialists generally expect the millennium to last throughout the church age; therefore, it is believed to be indefinite in length rather than a literal thousand-year period.

4. Amillennialists expect the millennium to end when Christ returns. The final state will follow shortly after His return.

5. Amillennialists generally believe in the imminent or any-moment return of Christ. Some tone this down by using the word "impending" rather than "imminent". For example, Anthony a. Hoekema says, *"Instead of saying that the Parousia is imminent, therefore, let us say that it is impending."*[9]

6. Amillennialists often expect end-time persecution of Christians to intensify under an antichrist, beast, or man of sin, and that this persecution will end with a Christian victory at the so-called Battle of Armageddon or Battle of Gog and Magog. To the amillennialists, however, this may be a reality before one can be sure what is happening.

Intensified evil near the end does not affect the heavenly millennium of most amillennialists, as is the case with those systems advocating an earthly millennium.

7. Amillennialists have divided expectations concerning a future conversion of Israel. While all believe Jews are going to be saved throughout the church age, all are not sure of an end-time national conversion. All saved Jews, regardless of when they are converted, are considered a part of the church. There is no separate plan for Israel apart from the church.

8. Amillennialists interpret Daniel's 70th week of prophecy as presently fulfilled. The 70th week followed the 69th in logical sequence. Any end-time tribulation is not to be connected with Daniel's prophecy, and it will not likely be seven years in duration.

9. Amillennialists, like postmillennialists, expect a General Resurrection, a General Judgment, and the final state of both saved and lost to follow closely thereafter.

10. Amillennialists interpret Revelation 20:4-6 a little differently from postmillennialists. While postmillennialists usually interpret it exclusively as a martyr scene but sometimes include all saints, amillennialists do the opposite. They generally apply it to all saints but occasionally restrict it as a martyr scene. The first resurrection is usually interpreted as the souls of saints being raised from earth to Heaven to live in a more quality way with Christ. The second resurrection is bodily and includes all people, saved and lost. Sometimes the first resurrection is said to be the new birth. Jay Adams holds that the first resurrection refers to something special given to Christian martyrs, while the second resurrection refers to all other non-martyred Christians.[10] It is more commonly believed,

however, that the millennium of Revelation 20:4-6 is a heavenly reign of souls with Christ.

11. Most amillennialists hold that many of the prophecies which both premillennialists and postmillennialists claim are to be fulfilled during an earthly millennium will actually be fulfilled in the new Heaven and earth. These amillennialists believe that it is in this eternal state, rather than during an earthly millennium, that the curse of nature will be lifted, the wolf and the lamb will lie down together, and the earth shall be full of knowledge of the Lord as the waters cover the sea (see Isa. 11:9; 65:17,25).

Chapter Summary

It is hoped that this chapter overview of millennialism will lead to a better understanding of not only the three main systems of thought, but the options that are available in each. The purpose of this chapter is not to prove but to compare. Obviously, all these millennial viewpoints cannot be correct. Hopefully this chapter will lead to a clearer understanding of arguments and proofs as presented in the following chapters.

Chapter 2

Prophecy and Hermeneutics

Hermeneutics Defined

Hermeneutics is the science of Biblical interpretation. What does this have to do with eschatology? It is the center of the problem; it is the principle determining factor in the choice of a millennial view.

Smoke Screens

Students of eschatology are bombarded with a number of smoke screens which should be removed before dealing with the real issue- hermeneutics. First, there is the smoke screen of those who believe a particular millennial view. Premillennialists often accuse others, especially amillennialists, of being bedfellows with Augustine and the Roman Catholic Church. They evidently hope that once they have put this label on amillennialists, their readers will not desire to give any consideration to such eschatology. Amillennialists and other non-premillennialists accuse the premillennialists of being bedfellows with Mormons, Jehovah's Witnesses, and others frequently referred to as cults. This is not the real issue; truth is not determined by who believes something.

The second smoke screen concerns the time a particular millennial view originated or developed. Each millenarian, of course, believes that his/her view originated in Biblical teachings. Premillennialists say that amillennialism originated with Augustine and the early Roman Catholic Church while the amillennialists claim dispensational premillennialism did not exist until about 1830 when it was first proclaimed by the Brethren Movement and John N. Darby. Again, truth is not determined by when a particular doctrine originated. The doctrine of the Trinity has always been true but was not fully developed and accepted until the Council of Nicaea in A.D. 325.

The third smoke screen centers on the number of adherents who accept a particular millennial view. Amillennialists, including Catholics, frequently point out that they far exceed premillennialists in numbers. Some premillennialists then respond by culling out all those they claim teach a false doctrine, and, when the culling process is over, premillennialists are about all that is left. Regardless of the accuracy of any of these claims, truth is not determined by numbers. Christ certainly proclaimed a minority doctrinal view during His earthly ministry.

The fourth smoke screen centers around the accusation of liberalism. Premillennialists sometimes claim there are liberals among both amillennialists and postmillennialists. The accusation is made to sound as if premillennialists are Bible believers while their opponents are not. This is simply another way to encourage the public not to give any consideration to either amillennialism or postmillennialism. Liberalism, however, is not the issue since one can be conservative in theology and adopt any one of the millennial systems. Premillennialists certainly have no exclusive possession of orthodoxy.

Rules of Hermeneutics

There are other smoke screens, but the real issue centers around hermeneutics. The Bible cannot be understood without first being interpreted. The big question then is what method or methods should be employed when interpreting the Bible. Must the Bible be interpreted literally, spiritually, or both ways? How do we determine which method or combination of methods should be used? This author believes that the following rules of interpretation, if followed, would lead to a more accurate Biblical understanding:

1. The Word of God, including prophecy, should be interpreted literally wherever possible, that is, when it will harmonize with the other rules of interpretation. Prophecy especially that of the apocalyptic type, will frequently have to be interpreted figuratively. Premillennialists often claim they interpret the Bible literally while others spiritualize its meaning away. In spite of claims to the contrary, there are no pure literalists or spiritualists. The idea of a single hermeneutic is nothing but a myth. The only difference lies in when, where, and how often one interprets literally or spiritually. How frequently and in what passages one literalizes or spiritualizes is what determines which eschatological view a person will ultimately adopt.

Dispensationalists are literalists only when it does not conflict with their presuppositions. They are the ones who teach there is no literal resurrection in Daniel 12:2, that the word "hour" in John 5:28 does not mean a literal hour but covers hundreds of years, that the word "all" in the same passage does not mean all, that the word "souls" in Revelation 20:4 does not mean souls but physical bodies, etc. These same interpreters are eager to proclaim that the seven churches of Revelation 1-3 are each symbolic of some church age. Then they claim that when John in his vision was called up into the heavens to receive his revelation, the passage was actually teaching that there would be a rapture of the church (Rev. 4:1). Of course, it is their system which demands this figurative interpretation because according to it the church cannot be present during the tribulation pictured in Revelation 4-19. After frequently interpreting the Bible this way, they turn around and remind others that they should take the Bible for what it says.

William E. Cox stated this first principle well when he said, "…An axiom of Bible study is that most sections demand literal interpretation unless the context or other known scripture passages demand figurative or spiritual interpretion."[1]Amillennialists place great emphasis on interpreting the Bible contextually. Floyd Hamilton when speaking on how the Bible should be interpreted commented:

But if we reject the literal method of interpretation as the universal rule for the interpretation of all prophecies, how are we to interpret them? Well, of course, there are many passages in prophecy that were meant to be taken literally. In fact, a good working rule to follow is that the literal interpretation of the prophecy is to be accepted unless (a) the passages contain obviously figurative language, or (b) unless the New Testament gives authority for interpreting them in other than a literal sense, or (c) unless a literal interpretation would produce a contradiction with truths, principles, or factual statements contained in non-symbolic books of the New Testament.[2]

2. Passages of Scripture that are clear and plain should carry more weight in formulating doctrine than passages in symbolic or figurative books such as Daniel and Revelation. All passages are inspired, but the true meaning of some is much more difficult to determine. Interpretation of an obscure passage should be influenced by the clear and plain passage rather than vice versa. For example, one passage in the highly symbolic book of Revelation should

not force one to go back and reinterpret the rest of the Bible. Revelation 20:1-6, which stands alone in teaching a millennium, should be interpreted in the light of the rest of the Bible. One passage, however, is enough to establish a doctrine if it is clear and plain, but no single passage should be interpreted in a way that is contradictory to other passages.

3. Old Testament prophecy should be interpreted in light of the more completed revelation of the New Testament. The Old Testament is a Jewish document written in Jewish language; the New Testament is a universal document written in Christian terminology but retaining a Jewish flavor. Without the New Testament, many Old Testament prophecies, presently fulfilled, would continue to lie in mystery. For example, Matthew claims that Zechariah 9:9 was fulfilled when Jesus rode a donkey into Jerusalem (Matt. 21:1-11). Since Jesus was not a literal king of the type that Jews expected, National Israel rejected this fulfillment. Christians, on the other hand, are able to see the fulfillment of Zechariah's prophecy since it is revealed in the New Testament.

Peter claims that Joel's prophecy, including the outpouring of the Holy Spirit in the last days (Joel 2:28-32), was fulfilled at Pentecost (Acts 2:19, 20). We know, therefore, from New Testament revelation that Old Testament prophecy concerning the last days covers at least the entire New Testament church age, not just events immediately preceding the return of Christ. Thus, where possible, we let the New Testament interpret the Old Testament. Peter continues with the Old Testament prediction that a king would someday sit on David's throne (Ps. 16:8-11) and declared it fulfilled by Christ sitting presently on David's throne in Heaven (Acts 2:30, 31). All millenarians ought to accept this.

Paul claims that the promise made to Abraham and his seed that through him all nations would be blessed (Gen. 18:18) has been fulfilled spiritually by Gentiles placing their faith in Christ (Gal. 3:8). The promise, therefore, was not to be fulfilled through his literal or fleshly seed but in his spiritual or faith seed. This New Testament interpretation should be accepted. These are only a few of the many examples of New Testament writers interpreting Old Testament prophets in a non-literal way.

The New Testament even at times repeals instructions, ordinances, rituals, etc. of the Old Testament. When the New Testament Book of Hebrews teaches that the old Temple system of sacrifices is forever replaced, then Ezekiel 40-48 should be interpreted in the light of this. If premillennialists would abide by this rule, then they would not have to look for a future literal fulfillment of Ezekiel's Temple prophecy.

4. Parallel passages should always be interpreted harmoniously. If one parallel passage in the four Gospels gives added information, then the other parallel passages should never be interpreted to contradict that revelation. For example, in the Olivet discourse, Luke reveals that the desolator of Jerusalem would be the soon-coming Roman army (Lk. 21:20). Parallel accounts in Matthew (Matt. 24:15) and in Mark (Mk. 13:14) which do not name the desolator should not be interpreted as referring to some future antichrist. Interpreting Luke as referring to A.D. 70 and Matthew and Mark to an event yet future violates a basic hermeneutical principle. All three parallel accounts must have the same meaning.

5. The context of a passage largely determines if it is to be interpreted literally or symbolically. Unlike history, prophetic language is often poetic and symbolic. For example, when Isaiah promised the Babylonian exiles that

the hills would become a plain and the rough country would be made smooth (Isa. 40:4), they were not supposed to interpret that literally. Also, when Jeremiah sees mountains trembling and hills moving to and fro (Jer. 4:23), he is speaking symbolically. To interpret him otherwise would be to miss the prophet's meaning. Scripture, therefore, must be interpreted according to its local context, to its book context, and in harmony with the context of the whole Bible. Scripture must be compared with Scripture because the Bible is its own best interpreter.

6. When interpreting Scripture, the simplest and most natural interpretation should be considered first. The order is always from the simple to the complex. The simplest interpretation will more likely be the correct one. Premillennialists are forced to assume the complex. Before interpreting a passage, they must ask which coming, which resurrection, which judgment, which dispensation, etc. Until the simpler is disproved, it should be allowed to stand.

7. Biblical prophecy is conditional even though the conditions are not always stated. Prophets at times predicted future conditions in order to get people to properly respond to the promise or threat. For example, Jonah was told to prophesy the downfall of Nineveh within a specified time and without any conditions attached. When the people of Nineveh responded to the prophet's message by repenting, the downfall did not occur as Jonah had predicted. The Lord, instead, decided to spare the city. Should Jonah be considered a false prophet because there was no literal fulfillment of his prophecy? No, he was a successful prophet rather than a false one. Conditions have to be understood even when not expressed. Blessings were predicted for Israel as long as she was faithful. When she became unfaithful, however, the tone of prophecy changed.

We are frequently reminded by hyper-literalists that God promised Abraham and his blood seed the land of Palestine unconditionally forever. If that were true, why have the Jews spent most of their history in other lands since that promise? Esau, a blood seed of Abraham, was excluded from this covenant because of disobedience. Why, if there were no conditions attached, did this happen? What literalists sometimes fail to understand is that conditions are understood even when not expressed. For example, when Jesus predicted that the kingdom would nationally be taken from the Jews and given to a nation that would bear fruit, he was implying that conditions were involved (Matt. 21:43). They should have been bearing fruit, but they were not.

8. The Bible itself testifies that prophecy is not always literally fulfilled. The first Biblical prophecy about Christ (Gen. 3:15) was never literally fulfilled. If Genesis 3:15 were literally fulfilled, a literal descendant of Eve would use his heel to bruise the head of a snake, and the snake in turn would have to strike the heel of its enemy. Christ, in dealing with Satan, fulfilled this substantially, but not literally.

Many prophets, including Moses, Jeremiah, and Ezekiel, predicted that the Israelites would find a land which flowed with milk and honey, but no one has reported finding any literal streams of either product. Neither do we hear anything about their prophecy having been only partially fulfilled with a complete fulfillment coming in the future. It was simply symbolic language describing a fruitful land.

Isaiah predicted the fall of Babylon in terms describing great physical destruction and loss of life (Isa. 13:14-22). Babylon, however, surrendered without the city being destroyed and apparently without resistance. The prophecy was fulfilled, but not literally in all details. Isaiah also predicted that the mountains were going to sing and the trees clap their hands (Isa. 55:12). Joel prophesied that the mountains would drop sweet wine and the hills would flow with milk (Joel 3:18). Daniel prophesied that Jerusalem would be destroyed by a flood (Dan. 9:26), but it was literally destroyed by a Roman army. These and many other prophecies were substantially but not literally fulfilled. When Christ told Nicodemus that he must be born again (Jn. 3:3), he being a literalist missed the proper interpretation. Those who always insist that prophecy be literally fulfilled are not observing the testimony of the Bible itself.

9. Old Testament prophecy is usually addressed to Israel as the covenant people of God, but may be fulfilled in the New Testament covenant people of God. The fact that they were Israelites was secondary to the fact that they were the covenant people of God. Peter addressing Christians said, "But ye are a chosen generation, a royal priesthood, a holy nation, a peculiar people…" (1. Pet. 2:9). No longer is the chosen covenant people with her priesthood and nationhood restricted to Jews. The church has replaced Israel as God's chosen people. Promises made to the Old Testament chosen people of God may be fulfilled in the New Testament chosen people of God.

Chapter Summary

It must be understood that Old Testament prophets had to communicate their message in language understandable to Israel. Predictions were made in language evolving around Jerusalem, the Temple, the sacrifices, the throne of David, etc. Otherwise, New Testament language and concepts would have been meaningless to the immediate audience of the prophets.

If this, along with the above rules of hermeneutics, were kept in mind when interpreting prophecy, the mistake of both hyper-literalizing and over-spiritualizing could be avoided.

Chapter 3

Prophecy and the Kingdom

The premillennial view of the kingdom is that it will at some future time be set up as a political and economic kingdom with Jerusalem as its center and Christ as its head. Exponents say it will last 1,000 years and that Christ will reign with a "rod of iron" type authority. There will be unparalleled peace and prosperity in fulfillment of Old Testament promises to Israel.

Some premillennialists, known as dispensationalists, argue that Christ intended to set up this kingdom at His first advent, but the Jews rejected His offer, and He had to postpone the kingdom until His Second Coming. They also maintain that the Kingdom of Heaven and the Kingdom of God are different. These dispensational concepts will be discussed later.

The postmillennial view of the kingdom is that it is spiritual in nature, that Christ presently rules in the hearts of Christians, and that the outward manifestation of the kingdom is the church. Postmillennialists are seeking to establish the kingdom in the hearts of people everywhere and believe they have Biblical reason to expect success. As the kingdom of Christ (Heaven or God) grows, the world will gradually get better with Christ reigning from Heaven. World conversion may not be absolute, but it will be the general rule.

Postmillennialism is the most optimistic of millennial views as far as kingdom growth is concerned. The church reigning triumphantly on earth by the authority of her heavenly King is believed to be the millennium. In contrast, the millennium of the premillennialists has Christ reigning on earth and ends up in worldwide rebellion. In time, however, the rebellion is put down, the earth is burned, the wicked are punished, and the righteous are rewarded.

The amillennial view of the kingdom is in many respects similar to the postmillennial view. They both believe that the kingdom is spiritual in nature, not political; they both believe that the kingdom is a present reality with Christ reigning in the hearts of Christians; they both see serious difficulties in any concept of a postponed kingdom with its many inherent errors; and they both agree that the Kingdom of Heaven and the Kingdom of God are interchangeable terms. Amillennialists, however, do not agree with postmillennialists who say there is Biblical support for a continuously improving world until it is finally Christianized. Neither do the amillennialists agree that a successful church is the millennium. To the amillennialists the millennium, found only in Revelation 20, is a heavenly scene and not an earthly one; it is not synonymous with the kingdom.

All millennial views agree that there is a sense in which the kingdom is future, but the agreement ends there. The premillennialist sees much Old Testament prophecy being fulfilled in a future earthly and political reign of Christ on earth. Postmillennialists see their prophecies being fulfilled on earth in a spiritual way during a glorious future age of the church while Christ reigns triumphantly from His heavenly throne. Amillennialists agree that as yet some Old Testament prophecies are not completely fulfilled but see their fulfillment in the eternal state or aspect of the kingdom. At such time the curse of nature will have been lifted on the new earth. Amillennialists often portray the kingdom as changing with time. They believe there WAS an Old Testament kingdom, and there WILL BE an eternal kingdom of God in the future. During the Old Testament kingdom the New Testament kingdom was thought of as future; under the present New Testament kingdom the eternal aspect of the kingdom is still future. This is really one kingdom in different stages.

How May the Kingdom Be Defined?

The preaching of the Kingdom of God was the central theme of Jesus, but He nowhere defined the meaning of the term. Neither did His apostles nor any other New Testament writes. The author of Romans told us what the Kingdom of God was not when he said, "For the kingdom of God is not meat and drink; but righteousness, and peace, and joy in the Holy Ghost" (Rom. 14:17). That was obviously not an exact definition.

It is generally conceded that the word "kingdom" is not always used in exactly the same way. Therefore, it is not easy to give a simple definition which pleases everyone. By induction from the Scriptures we may say that the Kingdom of God is the reign of God in Heaven or on earth. Through Jesus Christ, history is being directed toward its divine goal. He is saving people from their sins in spite of earthly and demonic powers; He will destroy this world (as we know it) when He chooses. A New Heaven and a new earth will be established. The kingdom, therefore, means that Christ is active in world affairs, and, while He chooses to respect the free will of man, He will continue to reign; the King will not be defeated. Heaven is His throne and the earth is His footstool.

This spiritual type reign of Christ, rather than a political or territorial one, is the central idea of the kingdom.

The Kingdom of God is large enough in scope that it can mean nothing less than the reign of God over the entire universe - Heaven and earth. Those who enter the kingdom by a new spiritual birth reign with Christ; those who reject the King will ultimately be judged and punished. It matters not if one is black or white, male or female, Jew or Gentile, young or old, rich or poor, educated or uneducated; if he has been born of God, he is presently a citizen of the kingdom. When Jesus proclaimed the Kingdom of God, He proclaimed spiritual salvation. The spiritual aspect is always more important than the physical.

Has the Kingdom Been Postponed?

According to dispensationalists, the kingdom has been postponed. Since they believe that a visible earthly kingdom has been promised to the Jews and since that kingdom was announced as being "at hand" by both John the Baptist and Christ, there has to be some explanation for its not being established. M.R. Dehaan explained it by saying, "…The kingdom of heaven is the reign of heaven's King on earth. This Jesus offered to the nation of Israel when he came the first time, but they rejected it and he went to the cross."[1] W.E. Blackstone when speaking of the kingdom being "at hand" said, "But the Jews rejected it and slew their King. They were not willing to have this man reign over them, and therefore, the Kingdom did not immediately appear."[2] Blackstone further states, "The Kingdom did come 'nigh' when Jesus came, and had they received Him, it would have been manifested, but now it is in abeyance, or waiting until He comes again."[3] Hal Lindsey, another dispensationalist, commented:

Jesus was indeed the long-awaited Messiah. Had the people received Him, he would have fulfilled the kingly prophecies in their day in addition to the ones regarding the suffering Messiah. But when the Jewish nation as a whole rejected Christ, the fulfillment of His kingship was postponed until the final culmination of world history.[4]

The dispensational view is that the kingdom was REJECTED by the Jews and POSTPONED by Christ. This seems to make both the death of Christ and the church afterthoughts of God. S.D. Gordon stated it very strongly when he affirmed:

It can be said at once that His dying was not God's own plan. It was a plan conceived somewhere else and yielded to by God. God had a plan of atonement by which men who were willing could be saved from sin and its effects.[5]

Apparently, S.D. Gordon is saying that the purpose of the manger was not the cross. God already had a plan of atonement sufficient to save Jews, the Jewish system of sacrifices. If this were true and they had a kingdom that was eternal, they could have continued indefinitely to offer their sacrifices as an atonement. Only after God's first plan was rejected did He offer a second. Accordingly, God did not plan on the death of Christ, but when the Jews rejected Him, the kingdom had to be postponed.

Postponement carried to its logical conclusion teaches that the cross was not necessary. Loraine Boettner expressed it well when he said, "According to this view Christ's atonement for the sins of the world became necessary only because His original plan miscarried."[6] Therefore, the mystery of the church based upon the cross came into play temporarily. The church is expected to soon be raptured out of the way, and then God will return to His original plan to set up a political earthly Jewish kingdom. How, may we ask, can we be sure that He will be able to do at His Second Advent what He could not do at His first?

On the postponement concept, dispensationalists stand alone; all others, including non-dispensational premillennialists, firmly reject the idea. The general tone of the Scriptures reject it also. Jesus contradicted the concept that He did not come to die when He said, "For even the Son of man came not to be ministered unto, but to minister, and to give his life a ransom for many" (Mk. 10:45). This same verse denies that the Jewish sacrificial system was sufficient as an atonement. The writer of Hebrews said, "For it is not possible that the blood of bulls and of goats should take away sins" (Heb. 10:4). That it was the plan of God for Jesus to die is everywhere taught in the Scriptures. Luke said "Him, being delivered by the determinate counsel and foreknowledge of God, ye have taken, and by wicked hands have crucified and slain" (Acts 2:23).

If the kingdom were postponed, as often claimed, then the kingship of Christ was of necessity postponed also. There can be no king without a kingdom. Hal Lindsey states, "But when the Jewish nation as a whole rejected Christ, the fulfillment of his kingship was postponed until the final culmination of world history."[7] Jesus, however, maintained His kingship to the end. He declared His kingship the week before He was crucified when He made His triumphal entry into Jerusalem as a king (Matt. 21:5). This is also said to be a fulfillment of Zechariah's prophecy of the kingship of the Messiah (Zech. 9:9, 10).

Christ later, when being questioned by Pilate, maintained that He was a king. Jesus said to Pilate, "My kingdom is not of this world: if my kingdom were of this world, then would my servants fight, that I should not be delivered to the Jews: but now is my kingdom not from hence" (Jn. 18:36). In spite of what other may say, Jesus maintained that His Kingdom was not of this world. When Pilate asked Jesus if He were a king, Jesus replied, "Thou sayest that I am a king. To this end was I born, and for this cause came I into the world..." (Jn. 18:37). This is surely to be interpreted as an affirmative answer. It satisfied Pilate for he declared, "I find in him no fault at all" (Jn. 18:38). Jesus, when arraigned before Pilate, was accused of treason by the Jews, but He denied that He was guilty. If He in fact intended to set up a political kingdom, it would have necessitated the over-throw of Rome. Yet, Christ maintained this was not His intention.

Instead of the kingdom being postponed, the Bible affirms that it was fulfilled in the spiritual seed of Abraham (Christians) rather than in the natural seed (Jews). Jesus when speaking to the Jews said, "Therefore say I unto you, the Kingdom of God shall be taken from you, and given to a nation bringing forth the fruits thereof" (Matt. 21:43). John the Baptist told the Jews that being the literal seed of Abraham was not sufficient (Matt. 3:9, 10), and Jesus told Nicodemus, "Verily, verily, I say unto thee, except a man be born again, he cannot see the kingdom of God" (Jn. 3:3). Jesus predicted the destruction of Jerusalem and the soon coming end of the Jewish economy (Matt. 23:37, 38). After Jesus spoke of the kingdom being taken from the Jews and of the end of the Jewish economy, He never hinted that it was ending only for a time known as the church age.

Are the Kingdom of Heaven and the Kingdom of God the Same?

These terms are interpreted as being synonymous by all millenarians except dispensationalists. Both terms occur frequently in the Bible, but Matthew is the only one who uses the term "Kingdom of Heaven." All other Bible writers use the expression "Kingdom of God." Even Matthew occasionally uses the term "Kingdom of God." Jesus used the terms interchangeably when He said:

Verily I say unto you, That a rich man shall hardly enter into the kingdom of HEAVEN. And again I say unto you, It is easier for a camel to go through the eye of a needle, than for a rich man to enter the kingdom of GOD (Matt. 19:23, 24).

Also three of the parables of Matthew 13 (the Sower, the Mustard Seed, and the Leaven) use the term *Kingdom of Heaven* while the parallel passages in Mark and Luke use the term *Kingdom of God*. For further proof that the terms are used interchangeably, the reader is encouraged to compare the following: Matthew 4:17 with Mark 1:15; Matthew 10:7 with Luke 9:2; Matthew 5:3 with Luke 6:20; Matthew 8:11 with Luke 13:29; Matthew 11:11 with Luke 7:28; Matthew 13:11 with Mark 4:11; Matthew 13:31 with Mark 4:30; and Matthew 19:14 with Mark 10:14. In spite of this proof, dispensationalists maintain that the Kingdom of Heaven means the Messianic rule of Christ on earth in fulfillment of Old Testament promises to Jews, while the Kingdom of God means God's rule in hearts everywhere at all times. They contend that the Kingdom of Heaven was postponed, while the Kingdom of God is a present reality. This dispensational view, therefore, hinges on an alleged distinction in terminology; a distinction that simply does not exist. This alleged distinction makes the present church age a part of the Kingdom of God but not a part of the Kingdom of Heaven. It is clear, however, that Christ gave to Peter the keys to the Kingdom of Heaven when He said to him, "And I will give unto thee the keys of the kingdom of heaven..." (Matt. 16:19). If the Kingdom of Heaven is not now in existence, then it follows that Peter did not get to use the keys. Peter did, however, use these keys to open the door of salvation to the Jews on the Day of Pentecost (Acts 2) and later to the Gentiles (Acts 10). If Jesus and the Gospel writers used these two terms (Kingdom of heaven and Kingdom of God) interchangeably, we may safely do so and not worry about any differences of meaning. Such hairsplitting distinctions are unwarranted and non-biblical.

Are the Gospel of the Kingdom and the Gospel of Grace the Same?

Dispensationalists claim the gospel of the kingdom and the gospel of grace are two separate gospels. When the kingdom was postpones, the gospel of the kingdom was also postponed and will not be preached again until after the rapture of the church. Thus, a postponed kingdom led to a postponed kingship and a postponed gospel.

Clarence Larkin, a dispensationalist, once said, "...The gospel of the kingdom...is to be preached again after the rapture of the church for a witness unto all nations..."[8] Herschel Ford said, "A remnant of the Jews will preach the Gospel of the kingdom. Today we preach the Gospel of grace."[9] Dispensationalists in general portray the idea that the gospel of the kingdom is not being preached today. It was preached until the kingdom was postponed, then God through Paul revealed the gospel of grace. The body of Christ which resulted from the preaching of the gospel will be completed and raptured. Then the Jewish gospel of the kingdom will be preached once again.

According to this view, there are two separate gospels. The gospel of the kingdom was preached until the kingdom was postponed; during this present church age the gospel of grace is being preached; and after the church is raptured there will be a return to the gospel of the kingdom. But what does the Bible say? Paul said to the Galatians:

I marvel that ye are so soon removed from him that called you into the grace of Christ unto another gospel; Which is not another; but there be some that trouble you, and would pervert the gospel of Christ. But though we, or an angel from heaven, preach any other gospel unto you than that which we have preached unto you, let him be accursed. As we said before, so say I now again, if any man preach any other gospel unto you than that ye have received, let him be accursed (Gal. 1:6-9).

Even the casual reader of the Book of Galatians will conclude that Paul did not place any faith in Judaism. Without preconceived expectations it would never be thought of. The gospel of the kingdom, the gospel of grace, the gospel of Christ, or the gospel by any other name is simply one gospel. Christ has come and paid the price for sin. No Jewish gospel of the kingdom will ever save anyone, Jew or Gentile. The gospel of the kingdom is not some future return to Judaism, the only gospel that will ever save is the gospel of Christ.

Is the Kingdom Political or Spiritual in Nature?

Everyone agrees that John the Baptist and Jesus proclaimed that the kingdom was at hand. The question is, however, what type of a kingdom were they speaking of? Premillennialists believe it was an earthly political kingdom. Other millenarians believe it was a spiritual kingdom with Christ as its head.

When Christ first began to preach, He said, "Repent: for the kingdom of heaven is at hand" (Matt. 4:17). Repentance was thus a spiritual preparation. Jesus further stated, "Verily, verily, I say unto thee, Except a man be born again, he cannot see the kingdom of God" (Jn. 3:3). Here Jesus taught that a spiritual birth was essential to kingdom entrance. This would not be true if He were talking about a forceful political kingdom. It has previously been pointed out that Christ maintained before Pilate that His kingdom was spiritual in nature and not of this world. If Pilate had believed that Christ was a rival of Rome, he certainly would not have concluded, "I find in him no fault at all" (Jn. 18:38).

That the Jews generally expected an earthly political kingdom is not denied. That is what they wanted prophecy to say; and it, therefore, became easy to read this into prophetic passages. Had Christ, as is often claimed, come to set up a political kingdom, the Jews who expected and desired such a kingdom would surely have received Him. Their rejection of Christ is, therefore, proof that He never offered such a kingdom.

The truth is that after the Jews saw that Christ could heal all sicknesses and even raise the dead, they tried to force Him to become their king. They must have reasoned that with such a powerful king the fact that Rome had them greatly outnumbered was of little consequence. The miraculous supply of health, food, and life would offset any advantage Rome had over Israel. John declared:

Then those men, when they had seen the miracle that Jesus did, said, This is of a truth that prophet that should come into the world. When Jesus therefore perceived that they would come and take him by force, to make him a king, he departed again into a mountain himself alone (Jn. 6:14:15).

Christ rejected this offer of the Jews because they were interested in the physical while He was more interested in the spiritual.

The kingdom is sometimes referred to as the Kingdom of Heaven. This simply means that the nature of the kingdom is heavenly or of the nature of Heaven. Though the Jews did not as a whole realize it, such a spiritual kingdom would be far superior to any possible earthly kingdom, even one like that of David or Solomon.

Since the kingdom is spiritual and universal in nature, it cannot be established or advanced through war and bloodshed. We are in a war whereby we are admonished to fight, put on armor, have a breastplate, shield, helmet, and a sword (Eph. 6:11-17). This is, however, to be interpreted as a spiritual war rather than a literal one. The sword is the Word of God, and the spiritual kingdom is advanced through the proclamation of the Word of God. Love and peace, not force, characterize the kingdom of Christ.

Jesus further taught that His kingdom was not political in nature when He said, "My kingdom is not of this world…" (Jn. 18:36). The kingdoms of David and Solomon were of this world but not the kingdom of Christ. The author of Romans was also emphasizing the spiritual nature of the kingdom when he said, "For the kingdom of God is not meat and drink; but righteousness, and peace, and joy in the Holy Ghost" (Rom. 14:17). Any kingdom based upon race and not characterized by love, righteousness, peace, joy, etc. cannot be the Kingdom of God referred to in the New Testament.

The kingdom is not only spiritual but universal in nature. God does not care anymore for Jews than He does Gentiles. A spiritual birth is more important with God than race. Jesus had the universal scope of the kingdom in mind when He said, "For God so loved the world, that he gave his only begotten Son, that whosoever believeth in him should not perish, but have everlasting life" (Jn. 3:16). God did not simply love the Jewish world; neither did Christ die for the Jews only. Thank God, His kingdom was available on equal terms to every race. Peter, being a Jew, may have been slow to perceive the universal scope of the kingdom, but after a miracle from God, he said to the Gentiles, "Of a truth I perceive that God is no respecter of persons: But in every nation he that feareth him, and worketh righteousness, is accepted with him" (Acts 10:34, 35). In contrast to this Biblical concept, the whole idea of a future political reign of Christ with Jerusalem as His capital is built upon Jewish favoritism

While speaking to saved Gentiles, Paul said, "But now in Christ Jesus ye who sometimes were far off are made nigh by the blood of Christ. For he is our peace, who hath made both one, and hath broken down the middle wall of partition between us" (Eph. 2:13, 14). Jesus did not remove racial barriers temporarily; racial importance is gone forever. Jesus implied the same when He talked with the Samaritan woman at the well of Sychar (Jn. 4:23, 24).

With God's plan for the unity of the races in mind, Archibald Hughes very ably stated:

Every expression that once denoted the Israel of the Old Testament is, now and forever, invested with a new spiritual significance and applicable only to the true believer in the Lord Jesus Christ. The believers from Jews and Gentiles are now called Christians and are: The sons of Abraham (Gal. 3:7); Abraham's seed (Gal. 3:26-19); the Jew of the New Covenant (Rom. 2:28,29); the Circumcision (Rom. 2:28,29; Phil. 3:3); The Israel of God (Rom. 9:6-8); the Commonwealth of Israel (Eph. 2:12,13); The holy nation, the chosen generation, royal priesthood, peculiar people, the people of God (1 Pet. 2:9,10); The heirs of the promises (Rom. 4:16).[10]

It is, therefore, maintained that it was never God's plan to establish an exclusive Jewish kingdom during which Jews would reign supremely. It was His plan to establish a spiritual and universal kingdom. When Old Testament prophecies are interpreted in the light of the New Testament that is exactly what one finds.

What is the Time Frame of the Kingdom?

The kingdom was preached by John the Baptist, Jesus, and His disciples as being "at hand" (Matt. 3:2; 4:17; 10:7). It would seem that this was either true, or they were false prophets. Jesus said, "Verily I say unto you, That there be some of them that stand here, which shall not taste death, till they have seen the kingdom of God come with power"(Mk. 9:1). Jesus' kingdom, therefore, came during the lifetime of some of those to whom He spoke, or He was a false prophet. The postponement theory makes Christ a false prophet. Dispensational failure to understand that the kingdom prophesied in the Old Testament was to be fulfilled spiritually rather than politically necessitated the postponement idea.

A number of the parables of Christ also imply that the kingdom is already present. Two examples are the parable of Hidden Treasure (Matt. 13:44) and the parable of Goodly Pearls (Matt. 13:45).

The spiritual kingdom of Christ was manifested with power on the Day of Pentecost (Mk. 9:1; Lk. 24:29; Acts 1:8). According to the Bible, Christians were already in the kingdom during the first century A.D. for Paul said, "Who hath delivered us from the power of darkness, and hath translated us into the kingdom of his dear Son" (Col. 1:13). One cannot be translated into something that has been postponed and does not exist. John, when introducing the Book of Revelation, taught that he was already in the kingdom; he said, "I, John, who also am your brother, and companion in tribulation, and IN THE KINGDOM and patience of Jesus Christ, was in the isle that is called Patmos..." (Rev. 1:9).

While at Ephesus, Paul claimed to have taught the gospel and preached the Kingdom of God while a prisoner at Rome (Acts 28:23, 31). The spiritual kingdom which Christ came to set up was a present reality both then and now; people are born into this kingdom.

This does not mean that there is not a future aspect of the kingdom. Premillennialists emphasize that the future aspect will be political. Postmillennialists emphasize that the future aspect will be spiritual in nature with the church reigning triumphantly on earth before the return of Christ. Amillennialists emphasize the future aspect as being the eternal state or kingdom which shall exist after the creation of a new Heaven and a new earth.

On several occasions, Christ evidently has the future aspect of the kingdom in mind (Matt. 7:21-23; 8:11, 12; Mk. 14:25; Lk. 22:16, 18). Paul also made reference to the future aspect of the kingdom (2 Tim. 4:18; 1 Cor. 6:9, 10; Gal. 5:21; 1 Cor. 15:50).

The Biblical message is that Christians are now in the Kingdom of God, but the kingdom is presently in an incomplete state. The final and eternal state of the kingdom will be entered only after Christ returns, raises all the dead, judges the world, and creates a new Heaven and a new earth. In this final state, the kingdom will not co-exist with evil. We presently become part of the kingdom while still flesh and blood; in the final state, flesh and blood will not exist. Christ taught that in the final aspect of the kingdom there would be no marriage or sexual distinctions, but we would be as angles who do not procreate (Matt. 23:30; Mk. 12:25).

What About Old Testament Prophecy and the Kingdom?

It should not be necessary to spend a great amount of time in exegesis of Old Testament prophecies which predicted that Christ would come to establish a spiritual or moral kingdom rather than a political one. However, authors such as C. I. Scofeild, Clarence Larkin, H. A. Ironside, Lewis S. Chafer, Hal Lindsey, and others make it necessary to give some response. The present response is not intended to be exhaustive in nature but will deal with a few frequently used prophetic passages.

Perhaps the most often used passage is in support of a future political kingdom of Christ is found in the Book of Daniel; he affirmed:

And in the days of these kings shall the God of heaven set up a kingdom, which shall never be destroyed: and the kingdom shall not be left to other people, but it shall break in pieces and consume all these kingdoms, and it shall stand forever (Dan. 2:44).

This passage tells when (during the Roman Empire) the kingdom will be established and how long it will last (forever).

In the preceding verses of Daniel 2 is the story of King Nebuchadnezzar having a dream about a large image. This image had a head of gold which referred to Nebuchadnezzar himself and his Babylonian kingdom. The image also had other parts of a human body which pictured what was at that time future kingdoms. The Babylonian kingdom was to be followed by a Medo-Persian kingdom under men like Cyrus, and later a Grecian kingdom under men like Alexander the Great, and finally a Roman kingdom under the various emperors of Rome. It was during this Roman kingdom that yet another kingdom, unlike the previously pictured kingdoms, would be set up. While all the other kingdoms were materialistic and would each in its own time end, this last kingdom that was set up during the first advent of Christ. If Christ did not establish His kingdom, the prophecy of Daniel 2:44 failed. Stafford North was absolutely correct when he said, "The TIME predicted is as important a part of a prophecy as the EVENT; if the time aspect fails, the prophecy fails."[11]

On the other hand, a number of authors and speakers tell us that Christ did intend to establish His kingdom during the first Roman Empire but had to postpone it. To make the prophecy take place in a Roman Empire, though it would be the wrong one, these same people predict with certainty the rise of a yet future Roman Empire during which Christ will appear and set up a political kingdom that will last for 1,000 years. This is all supposed to be clear from Daniel 2:44.

Such reasoning results from a misunderstanding of the intent of the prophecy. Christ did set up His spiritual kingdom at the time He said He would. If the prophecy itself did not make clear whether the kingdom would be political or spiritual, time did.

Another prophetic passage often used as a proof text for a future political kingdom is found in Daniel 7. Here Daniel, in a vision, sees four beasts rise up out of the sea. The first was like a lion, the second was like a bear, the third was like a leopard, and the fourth was a ten-horned creature that was able to defeat the third. This was probably the same four kingdoms as those of the earlier visions of Daniel recorded in chapter 2. Rome is the ten-horned beast. The son of man (Jesus), however, appears and establishes an eternal kingdom (Dan. 7:13; 14,27) being even stronger than the ten-horned Roman Empire. Many, again, assume this prophecy can only be fulfilled by a political reign of Christ. Since He did not do this at His first advent, it is yet future. But what does this false assumption do to the passage?

Daniel says:

After this I saw in the night visions, and behold a fourth beast, dreadful and terrible, and strong exceedingly; and it has great iron teeth: it devoured and brake in pieces, and stamped the residue with feet of it; and it was diverse from all the beasts that were before it; and it had ten horns (Dan. 7:7).

This is the Roman Empire that was in existence at the first advent of Christ. A preconceived theory of a political kingdom causes a number of writers to divide the above verse leaving what is already a gap of approximately 2,000 years. They maintain that the Roman Empire of the first part of the verse is separated by a large gap from the ten-horned Roman Empire in the latter part of the verse. They claim that this verse teaches that two different Roman empires were in the mind of the prophet. There is, however, no hint of such a gap.

In Daniel 11 these interpreters of prophecy continue with their gap-type skipping of time, but such interpretation is surely unwarranted.

When interpreting Ezekiel's prophecy, the dispensationalists again postpone until some future period that which has already been fulfilled. Ezekiel prophesied to the Israelites in Babylonian captivity. At the beginning of the book, some Jews were still in Jerusalem, and Ezekiel's prophecy told of their actions leading to the destruction of Jerusalem which included Solomon's Temple. In the latter part of his book, Ezekiel encouraged the captives by predicting a return to their homeland and the rebuilding of a temple. This all happened and is now history.

Dispensationalists object to this and say there was a temple rebuilt, but the measurements were different from those predicted. We, therefore, are told to look to the future for a fulfillment of Ezekiel's prophecy. The exact measurements of the prophecy do not work very well for anyone including those who believe a yet future temple was in the mind of the prophet. Prophetic numbers need not be over literalized. Everyone knows, including dispensationalists, that a prophetic year may actually mean several years. This will be dealt with later when dealing with Daniel's 70 years of prophetic history. Some, not dispensational in theology, believe that Zerubbabel's Temple was smaller than Ezekiel's prophetic temple as a result of conditional elements not being fulfilled by Israel (Ezek. 43:10,11). Others believe the description should be understood in a spiritual sense, i.e., we are the temple of God (2 Cor. 6:16; Eph. 2:19-22). Regardless of the correct interpretation, it seems clear that it does not refer to some future temple with an Old Testament system of animal sacrifices reinstated.

Claiming the prophetic temple of Ezekiel 40-48 is yet future creates a serious problem for its advocates. It means a future return to animal sacrifices, a system abolished by the sacrifice of Christ and considered apostasy by the New Testament writes. To try and pass these sacrifices off as memorial in nature is a total departure from literal interpretations; there is absolutely no hint of any such memorial anywhere in the Book of Ezekiel. On the other hand, the sacrifices are always pictured with their traditional Old Testament significance. In the interest of space the reader is asked to read for himself about the prophetic temple with its animal sacrifices for sin (Ezek. 40:42; 42:13, 14; 43:19-27; 45:21, 25; 46:20). It should be noticed that Gentiles, at least without circumcision, were not to be allowed in this temple (Ezek. 44:9). This writer maintains that the Levitical priesthood has been eternally abolished (Heb. 7:11); and so has the rite of circumcision (Gal. 5:2). The real difficulty disappears if the prophecy is referred to Zerubbabel's Temple which was built following the Babylonian captivity while the Old Testament economy was still in effect. To apply it to a yet future temple is to negate the sacrifice of Jesus Christ.

Chapter Summary

What are the Biblical facts about the kingdom? Negatively, it is not some future political and economic government with headquarters in Jerusalem. Neither is the kingdom presently postponed. The kingdom is spiritual in nature, and it is a present day reality.

The present kingdom does, however, have a future aspect. It will be turned over to God the Father at the coming of a new Heaven and earth. The Old Testament passages that premillennialists claim will be fulfilled in a future earthly kingdom either have already been fulfilled or will be fulfilled in the new earth, rather than during a millennium. Much dispensational theology results from a misinterpretation of Old Testament prophecy. This misinterpretation leads to unbelievable prophetic speculation concerning Israel. The subject of Israel, therefore, will be explored in the next chapter.

Chapter 4

Prophecy, Israel, and the Church

The relationship of Israel and the church is an important part of eschatology. What one believes concerning this relationship certainly helps shape one's eschatological position. Several questions need to be answered; four important ones will be considered in this chapter. They are: 1) Does God have a separate plan for Israel and the church? 2) Is a future national conversion of Jews promised? 3) Was the church a mystery unforeseen by the prophets? 4) Is the present Israeli nation a fulfillment of prophecy?

Does God Have a Separate Plan for Israel and the Church?

Dispensational premillennialists invariably insist that God has a different plan for Israel and the church, i.e., God has two separate bodies. The two must always be kept separate; Israel does not mean the church, and the church does not mean Israel. Old Testament promises to His chosen people, Israel, cannot be fulfilled in His New Testament chosen people, the church. This concept, of course, leaves many Old Testament promises yet unfulfilled. Dispensationalists think of God's separate program for fleshly Israel as unconditional and eternal. This program was begun by promises made to Abraham but temporarily interrupted with the postponement of the kingdom.

The New Testament church as a separate body resulted from Jewish rejection of Christ, but God supposedly plans to rapture the church to Heaven and return to dealing with His first body, Israel. To non-dispensationalists this makes the church appear as an afterthought of God and the crucifixion of Christ as secondary, a plan which came into play only after the Jewish program temporarily failed.

Dispensationalists seem to imply Jews and Gentiles have separate eternal destinies; the Jews are to inherit the earth forever and the Gentiles Heaven forever. Lewis S. Chafer states it thusly:

The dispensationalist believes that throughout the ages, God is pursing two distinct purposes: one related to the earth with earthly people and earthly objectives involved, while the other is related to heaven with heavenly people and heavenly objectives involved.[1]

Charles C. Ryrie affirmed:

Premillennialists believe...that the promises made to Abraham and David are unconditional and have or will have literal fulfillment. In no sense have these promises made to Israel been abrogated or fulfilled by the church, which is a distinct body in this age having promises and a destiny different from Israel's[2]

Another dispensationalist, John F. Walvoord, expressed the distinction by saying:

Of prime importance to the premillennial interpretation of Scripture is the distinction provided in the New Testament between God's present purpose for the church and His purpose for the nation Israel,...The New Testament as well as the Old, however, makes clear that the nation Israel as such has its promises fulfilled ultimately in the future reign of Christ over them. At that time Israel will be His people and God will be their God.[3]

Others could be quoted, but the preceding examples are sufficient to establish the point that dispensationalists believe that the church and Israel are two distinct groups and that God has two separate programs for them. Is this a true or false concept?

Non-dispensationalists maintain this concept is both false and dangerous. The word *Israel* is not confined to Jews; in fact, the Israelites are so mixed with other nationalities until their status as a separate race is somewhat questionable. Furthermore, Paul used the term *Israel* to include Gentiles who had become new creatures in Christ Jesus. He said, "For in Christ Jesus neither circumcision availeth anything, nor uncircumcision, but a new creature. And as many as walk according to this rule, peace be on them, and mercy, and upon the Israel of God" (Gal.6:15, 16). It is obvious that the phrase "as many as walk according to this rule" includes both the circumcised and uncircumcised (Jews and Gentiles). These Jews and Gentiles who had become new creatures in Christ were then called "The Israel of God." The "Israel of God" is a further description of "as many as walk according to this rule."

The Israel of God or church simply means the chosen people of God. In Old Testament times, Jews were the chosen people of God, but in the New Testament era, Christians (Jews and Gentiles) have inherited that position. In other words, the church has replaced natural Israel as the chosen people of God. Promises made to God's chosen people in Old Testament times can be fulfilled in God's chosen people in New Testament times.

How do we know that Christians have replaced Israel as God's chosen? Peter speaking to Christians (Jews and Gentiles) said, "But ye are a chosen generation, a royal priesthood, an holy nation, a peculiar people; that ye should shew forth the praises of him who hath called you out of darkness into his marvelous light" (1 Pet. 2:9). It is obvious that Peter here took Old Testament expressions that often described Israel and applied them to the New Testament church. The church had now replaced Israel as the organ through which God would work. Peter made it plain that terminology which once applied only to the nation of Israel must now be applied to the church.

When commenting on 1 Peter 2:9, Anthony A. Hoekema asked, "If the New Testament church is now God's holy nation, what room is left for the future emergence (in the millennium, so it is claimed) of another 'holy nation' which will be distinct from the church?"[4]

The claim that Israel always means fleshly Israel and can never mean the church is, therefore, not in harmony with the New Testament. Neither is there truth in the claim that the Bible always intends to exclude Israel when speaking of the church. Paul taught that not all descendants of Israel were true Israelites (Rom. 2:23, 29; 9:6). He also taught that one did not have to be a physical descendant of Abraham in order to be part of "the Israel of God" (Rom. 9:24; Gal. 6:16).

Dispensationalists, while trying to prove that God has a separate program for Israel, often point out Old Testament promises made to the seed of Abraham. But this does not prove the point, for Abraham's spiritual seed includes Gentiles and His natural seed includes Ishmaelites. The New Testament message is:

There is neither Jew nor Greek, there is neither bond nor free, there is neither male nor female; for ye are all one in Christ Jesus. And if ye be Christ's, then are ye Abraham's seed, and heirs according to the promise (Gal. 3:28, 29).

It is clear that New Testament believers, Jews and Gentiles, are Abraham's seed and heirs of the Old Testament promises to the seed of Abraham. Thus the church has replaced Israel as the true seed of Abraham.

This is not intended to imply that God made no national promises to Israel. God, in the Old Testament, made two types of promises to Israel —national and spiritual promises. Israel's national promises have either been literally fulfilled or invalidated because she through disobedience failed to meet God's conditions of covenant promises. There will be a return to this concept later in this chapter. The spiritual promises are being fulfilled through all the spiritual seed of Abraham; that is, the church. The spiritual seed includes believing Gentiles (Gen. 18:18; 22:18; Rom. 4:17; Gal. 3:28, 29; Eph. 2:11-16).

The New Testament makes it plain that God has one body, not two. It says:

But now in Christ Jesus ye who sometimes were far off are made nigh by the blood of Christ. For he is our peace, who hath made both one, and hath broken down the middle wall of partition between us; Having abolished in his flesh the enmity, even the law of commandments contained in ordinances; for to make in himself of twain one new man, so making peace; And that he might reconcile both unto God in ONE body by the cross…(Eph. 2:13-16).

Notice the terminology "hath made both one," "one new man," and "one body." To suggest that Christ did this temporarily as an afterthought is to do an injustice to the crucified Christ. There is no hint that He will in a future Jewish millennium rebuild the "wall of partition" between Jews and Gentiles. The oneness of God's people is taught throughout the New Testament. While discussing Old Testament promises being fulfilled spiritually though the church, William Hendriksen notes:

The restoration of "the preserved of Israel" (Isa. 49:6) is fulfilled when the gospel is brought to the Gentiles (Acts 13:47). The enlargement of Zion's tent (Isa. 54:1-3) is fulfilled when the Gentiles accept Christ (Gal. 4:27). The new covenant promised by the Lord through his servant Jeremiah (Jer. 31:31-34) is the one which guarantees complete salvation to every believer- whether Jew or Gentile- through simple faith in Christ, apart from all ceremonial ordinances (Heb. 8:8-12; 10:16-20). ...In other words, when a prophecy is destined to be fulfilled in the new dispensation it is fulfilled according to the spirit of that new era.[5]

It is worthy of note, however, that the New Testament church did start out as a Jewish body. It was originally a Jewish body inheriting Jewish promises. Gentiles were slowly added to the church, first as a result of a vision of Peter (Acts 10) and later as a result of Paul's call to minister to Gentiles. These Jews and Gentiles formed the one body of Christ, and there is no Biblical evidence that God at some future time will return to a program with His body –Israel – after He has raptured His body –the church. What about all the Gentiles who dispensationalists claim will be saved through Jewish evangelism after the rapture? Will those Gentiles be part of the Jewish body or the church body? Are they to be saved the same way others were saved prior to the rapture or through a restored system of Judaism? What does a restored system of Judaism say for the atonement of Christ? Does not such a restoration destroy the real message of the Book of Hebrews?

Is a Future National Conversion of Jews Promised?

Premillennialists, postmillennialists, and part of the amillennialists say that a future national conversion of Jews is promised. When reasons are examined, however, the evidence is not as overwhelming as it at first may seem. Since premillennialism is a Jewish oriented system, it is natural for those who hold this view to interpret the whole Bible as an advocate of Jewish favoritism. Since postmillennialists believe in a future world conversion, they naturally expect Jews to be included. Some amillennialists, however, also believe that a future national conversion of the Jews is promised. This being true, it is clear that the belief in a future conversion of large numbers of Jews does not within itself determine one's millennial position. Where does this widespread idea of a future Jewish conversion come from? The usual answer is Romans 9-11.

Romans 9-11

A careful study of this passage will reveal that it is not necessary to conclude that it actually promises large scale Jewish conversion; the author deals more with possibility than probability. Such a possibility is based partially upon the statement, "And they also, if they abide not still in unbelief, shall be grafted in..." (Rom. 11:23). "If" is a big word, and it seems clear that the author of Romans actually expected only remnant salvation of the Jews. Room is left, however, for this to be a large remnant.

Nowhere in Romans 9-11 does God promise a national restoration of Israel to the land. This is often, however, read into the passage. Isaiah predicted that only a remnant of Israel would be saved; he is quoted in Romans as saying, "Esaias also crieth concerning Israel, Through the number of the children of Israel be as the sand of the sea, a remnant shall be saved' (Rom. 9:27). The following verse explains why most of the Jews, in contrast to the Jewish remnant, remained spiritually lost. Chapter 10 continues with the author desiring the spiritual salvation of national Israel but pointing out that it was not a reality.

Chapter 11 opens with an explanation of the fact that it was not God's fault that Israel as a whole was without spiritual salvation. Paul pointed out that he was indeed an Israelite and he possessed salvation. He was a part of the

Jewish remnant of all ages that had or would obtain salvation by the faith in Christ. Note that the theme of the whole passages is remnant rather than national salvation.

In Romans 11:7-10, the message is that those not of the remnant were hardened. According to the following verses this hardening resulted in a benefit to the Gentiles. The Gentiles were then warned not to be puffed up because if God broke off the Jewish branches, He could do the same to the Gentile branches.

Those who believe in a future national conversion of Jews sometimes read it into the expression "their fullness." Paul said, "Now if the fall of them be the riches of the world, and the diminishing of them the riches of the Gentiles; how much more their fullness?" (Rom. 11:12). While it may be difficult to determine exactly what Paul meant by the term "fullness," it is not difficult to determine what he did not mean. It could not mean national conversion because Paul was not talking about that. After using the expressing "fullness," he then said, "If by any means I may provoke to emulation them which are my flesh, and might save SOME of them" (Rom. 11:14). Note the expression "might save some of them." Paul in the overall context of Romans 9-11 and in the immediate context of Romans 11 spoke of remnant salvation. He naturally desired that this remnant would experience great growth.

It is stated in the following verse, "For if the casting away of them be the reconciling of the world, what shall the receiving of them be, but life from the dead?" (Rom. 11:15). The "receiving of them" cannot refer to a future national conversion of Jews. In its context Paul had just referred to trying to "save some" through his preaching. Since these branches had already been cut off, their being grafted back into the olive tree at any point in history would be "life from the dead."

The next several verses picture the branches from one tree being grafted into another thereby creating a new unity. This is not simply a future event but something that has been taking place all along (Rom, 11:16-22).

In verse 23 God does make a promise to the Jews, but it is conditional. The promise is, "And they also, if they abide not still in unbelief, shall be grafted in..." (Rom. 11:23). The word "if" is a qualifier; the Jews will determine their own destiny. They must believe in Christ just like Paul did; there is no hint of a future special Jewish program that will be liberal enough to rescue them in another manner. The Book of Romans reveals that the door is open to the Jew on the same basis it is to the Gentile.

The expression, "That blindness in part is happened to Israel, until the fullness of the Gentile be come in" (Rom. 11:25), does not unconditionally promise a future national conversion. The Greek word "*achri* or *achris*" is translated "until," but here it does not mean that something else will happen after that. One of many possible examples of this truth comes from this same book. Paul said, "For until the law sin was in the world..." (Rom.5:13). Would anyone dare say that the word "*archi*" translated as "until" means that sin did not exist after the giving of the law? The "fullness of the Gentiles" referred to in verse 25 simply means when the full number of those being saved is completed and this will not take place until the consummation. A partial blindness of the Jews will also continue up to the consummation. That is all Paul is saying; he is not talking about what will happen after the consummation. Paul is not pointing to a date in world history; he is pointing to the end of history as we know it. This interpretation is in harmony with Paul's theme of remnant Jewish salvation throughout Romans 9-11.

The principle passage used as proof that God has promised a future national Jewish conversion is found in the next verse. It says, "And so all Israel shall be saved; as it is written, There shall come out of Sion the Deliverer, and shall turn away ungodliness from Jacob" (Rom. 11:26). Two primary questions are raised in this verse: 1) What is meant by the expression "all Israel"? 2) When did or shall the Deliverer appear to "turn away ungodliness from Jacob"; that is, Israel?

There are three principle views concerning the meaning of the expression "all Israel." According to the first view, "all Israel" refers to the nation of Israel as it will exist at the end-time. Those holding this view, however, do not teach that the national conversion will happen at the same time, in the same way, or through the same program. Those holding this view include dispensational premillennialists with their kingdom gospel and special Jewish program, the historical premillennialists, and still others who are not premillennial at all.

This end-time concept of the last Jewish generation being converted does not do justice to the term "all Israel." The literalists conveniently depart from their proclaimed literalism. At best the last generation of Jews will be only a tiny portion of the total number of Jews who have lived. Does this tiny fragment equal "all Israel?" Such an interpretation, however, is to be preferred over any literal interpretation that would in some way provide universal salvation to the Jews of all ages. Neither explanation is tenable for this verse. "Israel" at times may mean the total of fleshly Israel but not in this passage.

Furthermore, Paul did not say, "And THEN all Israel will be saved"; instead he said, "And SO all Israel will be saved." He was talking about the way and not simply the time when "all Israel" would be saved. He had earlier in the chapter described this way of people being saved as Gentile conversion resulting from Jewish unbelief and in turn Jews being saved as a result of jealousy over Gentile conversions. Paul could have had this in mind, or he might have been thinking of faith in Christ. In either case, he was not picturing an exclusively end-time event but something that was happening all along in history. It was even happening in Paul's day in small numbers rather than large numbers (Rom. 11:14).

The second view of the meaning of "all Israel" is that it refers to all the saved of God throughout history including both Jews and Gentiles. The word "Israel" is not restricted to Jews; neither is Israel's conversion restricted to the end-time. One of the better known exponents of this view was John Calvin. Calvin and other like scholars were right in giving Biblical proof that the term "Israel" could and often did include converted Gentiles. Their argument that the olive tree represented true Israel which included both Jews and Gentiles is also weighty especially since it is within the general context of Romans 11. It is true that the Bible elsewhere at times gives a spiritual connotation to the word "Israel" as used in this passage. In spite of the merit of this second view, there yet appears to be a more satisfactory explanation.

The third view is that the term "all Israel" in this passage refers to all Jewish believers, a body yet to be completed. In other words, it is the sum of all saved Jews collected throughout history, not simply Jewish believers of the end-times. It is all believing Israel rather than all national Israel. The word believing is added because of both the overall and immediate context.

What is the context? In Romans 9-11 Paul pictures himself as saved and part of the Jewish remnant while Jews are pictured as being lost. Were the Jews lost because God had completely rejected Israel (Rom.11:1)? Paul argued that they were not and offered himself (v. 1) and a remnant (v. 5) as proof. Lost Jews had been rejected because of their unbelief, not because of a divine decree. The rejection of Israel was, therefore, not complete or total (Rom. 11:14). Jews could be saved even in large numbers "if they abide not still in unbelief" (Rom. 11:23). This is an explanation of choice or freedom of the will. According to Romans 11:25, a partial blindness of Israel is to last until (not beyond but as long as) "the fullness of the Gentiles," i.e., until the total number of all saved Gentiles is completed. In contrast with the expression –"fullness of the Gentiles" –is the expression in the next verse, "And so all Israel shall be saved."

The words "all Israel" would have to refer to believing Israel since all fleshly Israel could not possibly be saved. Such a doctrine would violate the whole of Biblical teaching, the whole context of Romans 9-11, and the immediate context of the verse under consideration.

Paul's language "the fullness of the Gentiles be come in" refers to the final completion of the saved from among the Gentiles (v. 25), while his language "And so all Israel shall be saved" (v.26) refers to the final completion of the saved from among the Jews. This will happen at the same time; both will be completed when Jesus comes again. To teach that people will be saved after the return of Christ is anti-biblical. This will be dealt with later.

Some will object and appeal to the rest of verse 26 as proof that the "Deliverer" will yet save natural Israel from her sins. The whole verse reads, "And so all Israel shall be saved: as it is written, There shall come out of Sion the Deliverer, and shall turn away ungodliness from Jacob (Rom. 11:26). Paul is quoting Isaiah (see Isa. 59:2) who himself was probably paraphrasing David (see Ps. 14:7). The prophecy refers to the first and not the Second Coming of Christ; it was future tense for David and Isaiah but not for Paul. Jesus came as the Deliverer at His first coming; He will not come as Deliverer at His Second Coming but as a judge. This is the message of the Scriptures everywhere; nowhere does the Bible picture Christ coming a second time to save people. Romans 11:26 should not be interpreted so as to make it conflict with the whole of Biblical teaching.

In conclusion, Romans 9-11 does not teach the concept that Jews are still the chosen people of God nor that Gentiles are relatively unimportant. Neither does it state that God is totally finished with Jews. It does teach that a Jewish remnant has, is, and will continue to be saved. Paul does not contradict Jesus and teach that they will be saved after His return. Christ taught that at His return the door of salvation would be shut against any who would seek to enter (Matt. 25:10). The Bible message in general is that now is the time to be saved and that it will be impossible to do so after Christ returns. Paul taught that Jews and Gentiles who believe in Christ were presently being grafted into the same olive tree or body. God only has one body and one program. Both Jews and Gentiles will continue to be added to this one body until the consummation. Then the fullness of both groups which compose the one body of Christ will be completed. In essence that is the message of Romans 9-11.

Is the church a Mystery – Parenthesis?

According to dispensational premillennialists, the church is a mystery - parenthesis. Remember that their system is unique in that it claims God has a program with national Israel that is totally different from His program with the church; the two never mix. One has a heavenly destiny while the other has an earthly destiny. The church is a parenthesis rather than God's main program. Accordingly the church was established in order to fill a gap between the postponement and reinstatement of God's main program.

After the church age is finished, then God will return to His beloved Jewish program.

Dr. Chafer explains:

It should be observed that though Judaism and Christianity have much in common, they never merge the one into the other. Having each its own eschatology reaching on into eternity....The word of God distinguishes between earth and Heaven, even after they are created new. Similarly and as clearly it distinguishes between God's consistent and eternal heavenly purpose which is the substance of Christianity, and it is as illogical and fanciful to contend that Judaism and Christianity ever merge as it would be to contend that Heaven and earth cease to exist as separate spheres.[6]

It seems that those who follow these concepts to their logical conclusion teach that the church was unforeseen, temporary, and unnecessary. Since the church is temporary, her plan of salvation is temporary. Judaism with its legal obedience would have been sufficient if Christ had not been rejected. The cross was not necessary, and after this parenthesis church age is over, there will be a return to Judaism with its Temple, sacrifices, etc. The prophecies that dispensationalists quote never hint otherwise. There will be no cross in this kingdom gospel in contrast to the gospel of grace that is operative during the church age. The dispensational system seems to say that salvation came by legal obedience in Old Testament times, is obtained by grace through faith in Jesus Christ during the church age, and will come by legal obedience again after the church age. For example, Dr. Chafer says:

In light of these seven "present truth" realities we are enabled to recognize how great is the effect of the change from "the law which came by Moses" and "grace and truth which came by Jesus Christ." And when these changed conditions have run their course, we are assured that there will be a return to the legal kingdom grounds and the exaltation of that nation to whom pertains the covenants and promises.[7]

S.D. Gordon stated the dispensationalist concept very positively when he said, "It can be said at once that His dying was not God's own plan. It was conceived somewhere else and yielded to by God,"[8] again he said, "There is no cross in God's plan of atonement."[9]

Dispensationalism pictures God's intended program as temporarily sidetracked. The small and relatively unimportant church age is pictured as a gap squeezed in between Daniel's 69th and 70th weeks of prophecy. Sixty-nine Biblical weeks of prophecy followed each other in logical order, and then suddenly the kingdom was temporally postponed. The result of this postponement was a timeout period known as the church age. God's prophetic clock then stopped when His Jewish program was sidetracked. He will not count time during this timeout church age. Daniel's 70th prophetic week is still future, but when it arrives, God will return to this Jewish program and start the clock running again. Before this can happen, however, the church has to be raptured out of the way. Is this a true picture of the church that Christ purchased with His blood? Did not His sacrifice replace forever the Jewish sacrificial system which was itself only a temporary type? Is there not a big confusion about what was designed to be temporary? Was Judaism not designed to merge into Christianity following the crucifixion of Christ?

Where does the idea that the church is a mystery, and interlude, or a parenthesis come from? Though many of today's writers may call the church a mystery, no Biblical writer ever called it a mystery. Not one Scripture can be found anywhere that says the church is a mystery. Paul is misinterpreted as saying the church was a mystery. What Paul did say was:

How that by revelation he made known unto me the mystery…which in other ages was not made known unto the sons of men, as it is now revealed unto His holy apostles and prophets by the Spirit; That the Gentiles should be fellow heirs, and of the same body, and partakers of His promise in Christ by the gospel (Eph. 3:3,5,6).

The mystery Paul speaks of is not the church itself but its racial composition. The mystery was that Christian Gentiles would be equal partners with Christian Jews. The middle wall of partition would be broken down, and they were supposed to become one body in Christ. That was a shocker as well as a mystery. Peter did not see this truth until after his housetop vision (Acts 10), and Paul did not conceive this truth until after his Damascus Road experience (Acts 9).

It was not a total mystery, however. It was not unknown to Abraham (Gen. 12:3; 22:18; Gal. 3:8), to David (Ps. 22:27; 72:17), to Isaiah (Isa. 19:23-27; 49:6), or to Joel (Joel 2:28,32). This mystery was predicted in the Old Testament but not accepted and understood. It was clothed in Old Testament language under figures of the land, the Temple, and the sacrifices; otherwise, it would have meant nothing to the Israelites of those days. The prophets used things known to picture the unknown church age. A clearer understanding must await New Testament revelation. This is true not only concerning the church, but it also applies to other subjects found in Old Testament prophecies.

Therefore, Paul did not at all teach that the church was a mystery. He taught that something about the church was a mystery and that mystery was not revealed as clearly in the Old as it is in the New Testament. Nevertheless, it was revealed to a few. It was clearly in the plan of God from all eternity past. (Eph. 3:11).

Neither was the mixture of Jews and Gentiles ever a mystery to our Savoir for He said, "I am COME a light into the world, that *whosoever* believeth on me should not abide in darkness" (Jn. 12:46). This was the eternal plan; God's program was not changed as a result of Jewish rejection of Christ; it was carried out as planned. The purpose of the manger was the cross. The church was designed to replace Old Testament Israel and the sacrificial system. Judaism with its shadows and types has already served its purpose and passed away forever. The church program is God's eternal program for Jew and Gentile alike. This takes nothing from the Jews individually; instead, it gives the atonement of Christ its due.

It was the Old Testament program that was parenthetical and temporary. Boettner commented:

Ritualism and legalism came to an end with the crucifixion of Christ, and salvation was made equally available for all nations and races. The New Testament age or Church age is therefore no parenthesis, no side issue, but the original divine purpose to which the Old Testament had led step by step.[10]

Is the Present Israeli Nation a Fulfillment of Prophecy?

Premillennialists believe that the present state of Israel is a fulfillment of prophecy but differ on particulars. Both postmillennialists and amillennialists say it is not, but they also differ on particulars. Dispensational premillennialists base their argument on three false assumptions: 1) that Israel is still God's chosen people with a separate program, 2) that the church cannot inherit promises made to national Israel, and 3) that Old Testament promises were often unconditional and must always be fulfilled literally. These concepts have already been refuted. In order to answer whether or not the present Israeli nation is a fulfillment of prophecy, it is necessary to examine two additional questions: 1) Were Old Testament land promises to Israel fulfilled in Old Testament times? 2) Were any New Testament land promises made to Israel?

1. Were Old Testament Land Promises to Israel Fulfilled in Old Testament Times?

If conclusive proof can be given that Israel has already inherited all the land promised to her, then obviously the present Israeli nation is not a fulfillment of prophecy.

First, there will be an examination of the Scriptures which dispensationalists claim prove that Israel never inherited all the land promised to her and that Israel is now beginning the process of complete fulfillment. Second, Scriptures will be given which prove that all land promised to Israel was literally inherited during Old Testament times.

In Isaiah 11:11,12, Isaiah said:

And it shall come to pass in that day, that the Lord shall set his hand again the second time to recover the remnant of his people, which shall be left, from Assyria and from Egypt, and from Pathros, and from Cush, and from Elam, and from Shinar, and from Hamath, and from the islands of the sea. And he shall set up an ensign for the nations, and shall assemble the outcasts of Israel, and gather together the dispersed of Judah from the four corners of the earth.

Isaiah prophesied before, not following, the Babylonian captivity. Dispensationalists point out that Isaiah promised a "second" recovery and that "second" recovery is now in progress. But present-day events have nothing whatsoever to do with this "second: recovery. The first recovery had taken place under Moses, a time period long before Isaiah. God used Moses to recover his people from Egyptian bondage. The "second" recovery referred to by Isaiah was the recovery from Babylonian captivity. It was fulfilled long ago when in stages the Jews returned from the dispersal caused by the Babylonian armies.

Dispensationalists also claim this could not have referred solely to a return from Babylonian captivity because the return was from many nations, one sea (singular), and to all four directions. Most of these nations do not exist today. In its context (Isa.11:14) the Philistines, Edomites, Moabites, and Ammonites are added to this list. The fact that a few would come from all these places is not hard to explain. Rather than be captured by Babylon, Jews dispersed in all directions. Jeremiah, against his will, ended up with a group of Jews who went to Egypt (Jer. 43:6,7). Also it is a known fact that in those days it was not uncommon to sell war-prisoners to anyone who would buy them. It is natural that all these widely dispersed people did not return at one time; many died without returning. The argument that Isaiah 11:11,12 refers to events of the end-time is not tenable.

This prophecy was fulfilled in the sixth century B.C. when a remnant of Jews returned in stages from captivity. Zerubbabel, Ezra, Nehemiah, and others led in the resettlement and rebuilding.

It is popular also to use Jeremiah as proof of an end-time fulfillment of land promises. Jeremiah said:

...And I will turn away your captivity, and I will gather you from all the nations, and from all the places whither I have driven you, saith the LORD; and I will bring you again into the place whence I caused you to be carried away captive (Jer. 29:14).

Where is any proof that this promise refers to any recent or yet future event? Jeremiah prophesied concerning Babylonian captivity. Consider the context of Jeremiah 29:14, and it is clear that the passage speaks of a return "after seventy years" (Jer. 29:10). Several verses prior to verse 14 make it clear that Jeremiah was talking about a sixth century B.C. return.

Dispensationalists present the prophecy of Zechariah as sure proof of Jewish land restoration in the end-time. Zechariah said, "Thus saith the LORD of hosts; Behold, I will save my people from the east country, and from the West Country; And I will bring them, and they shall dwell in the misdt of Jerusalem..." (Zech. 8:7,8). The basis of the argument is that Zechariah prophesied this after Zerbubbabel and others had already led a group out of Babylonian captivity. It, therefore, must refer to an end-time return.

This is not a valid argument, however. It is true that part of the Jews had already returned at the time of the promise, but Zechariah was trying to get others to return. About 50,000 returned in the first group of returnees (Ez. 2:64,65). Ezra responded to the challenge and led a second group of returnees to Jerusalem in about 458 B. C. (Ez. 7:1,6,12,13). The king would release any and all Jews who wanted to go with Ezra, but he would not force anyone to leave. Some Jews chose to remain, and they formed the background for the Book of Esther. Zechariah's prediction was fulfilled when Ezra led this second group of returnees to resume construction of the Temple (Ez. 5:1,2).

The principle passages of Isaiah 11:11,12, Jeremiah 29:14, and Zechariah 8:7-8 cannot be proved to have any references to present activities in Israel. The same can be said for other Scriptural passages sometimes used to support dispensational teachings (Deut. 30:1-10; 1 Ki. 8:46-52; Jer. 23:3,7,8; Ezek. 36:17-19,24).

George L. Murray accurately states:

Every promise which dispensationalists interpret as supporting a Jewish restoration is a promise given either before or during the time of Israel's captivity in Babylon, and refers either to that captivity and restoration or, under appropriate figures and symbols, to the gospel era, or to the ultimate setting up of that everlasting kingdom, which shall never be destroyed, which is neither Jews nor Gentiles, but new creations in Christ Jesus. ...To be sure, the nation was sovereignly chosen by God as the channel through which His oracles might be given to the world; but God no longer deals with them as a chosen nation, but as individual sinners to whom He offers salvation by Jesus Christ.[11]

Turning to the positive side, it may be asked what Scriptures prove that Israel did, in fact, inherit all the land that she was promised. The first promise was given to Abraham. He was told, "...Lift up now thine eyes, and look form the place where thou art northward, and southward, and eastward, and westward: For all the land which thou seest, to thee will I give it, and to thy seed for ever" (Gen, 13:14,15). Boundary lines are mentioned in this same Abrahamic Covenant. The covenant continues, "In the same day the LORD made a covenant with Abram, saying, Unto thy seed have I given this land, from the river of Egypt unto the great river, the river Euphrates" (Gen. 15:18). The exact people who would give up this land are named (Gen. 15:19-21), and they did exist there at that time. Those who claim Genesis 15:19-21 as being fulfilled at the end-times must resurrect and rebuild these ancient nations.

All of this covenant found its fulfillment in Old Testament times. The author of Deuteronomy declares, "And he brought us out from thence, that he might bring us in, to give us the land which he sware unto our fathers" (Deut. 6:23). The Bible further declares, "so Joshua took the WHOLE land, according to ALL that the LORD said..." (Josh. 11:23). Again the Bible affirms:

And the LORD gave unto Israel ALL the land which he sware to give unto their fathers; and they possessed it, and dwelt therein. There failed not ought of any good thing which the LORD had spoken unto the house of Israel, ALL CAME TO PASS (Josh.21:43,45).

The nationalists that were to give up the land (Gen. 15:19-21) surrendered it as predicted (Neh. 9:7,8). Abraham got what he was promised according to Nehemiah. The boundary lines describing the ultimate extent of the territory to be conquered were given in Genesis 15:18 and declared fulfilled in 1 Kings4:21, 24,25 and 2 Chronicles 9:26. In spite of what the Bible says, dispensationalists often remind the public that Israel never actually possessed all the land promised to them. It should be understood that whatever political agreements may be reached in the future concerning Israel's land, they will not result from promises made to Abraham, for those promises were fulfilled long ago.

Dispensationalists often point out that according to Genesis 13:15 Israel was promised the land "forever." Since their first possession of the land was not forever, Israel must look to the future for fulfillment of the promise. Non-dispensationalists generally answer this in one of two ways.

Some argue the promise was conditioned upon obedience, and Israel forfeited her right through disobedience (Ex. 19:5; Deut. 4:1,40; 8:1,19,20; 30:15-20). It may be true that the conditions were not stated in the original abbreviated covenant given to Abraham. The conditions were to be understood and stated later. God does not always give man an up-front explanation. Remember how Jonah predicted the destruction of Nineveh within 40 days with no conditions attached (Jon. 3:4). Evidently God never spelled out any conditions, but they were to be understood. Nineveh met the conditions, and the city was not destroyed in 40 days as Jonah had declared.

The second non-dispensational argument is that the word "forever" must be interpreted within a limited framework. God gave the sign of circumcision to Abraham and declared it an "everlasting covenant" (Gen. 17:13), but circumcision is of no spiritual value today (Gal. 5:2). The eternity of the old covenant ended when the old covenant ended; as long as the old covenant was in effect, circumcision was in effect. The limited framework was for the duration of the covenant. Under certain circumstances Hebrew servants were to serve their master "For Ever" (Ex. 21:6), but this meant only as long as they lived. Surely no one would claim this meant eternal servitude even beyond the grave.

The seven-day Passover Feast was given as an ordinance "for ever" (Ex. 12:14,17). How many Christians still keep it? In the same way the old Jewish priesthood was intended as an "everlasting priesthood" (Num. 25:13; Ex. 40:15). Also the fires on Jewish altars were to "never go out"; they were to "ever be burning" (Lev. 6:13).

These and other Biblical illustrations prove that the word "forever" must be interpreted within its limited context. When Abraham's covenant is interrupted in this light, there is no problem. There is, therefore, no necessity for all the land to be given back to the Jews so they can have it during the millennium and, in fact, in eternity after the land is made new. They have already possessed all the land as long as the contract was in effect. They were supposed to lose the land if and when they were disobedient (Deut. 4:1,23,26,27; 28:63,68). The present Israeli nation has nothing to do with making good a promise to Abraham.

2. Were Any New Testament Land Promises Made to Israel?

One will search the New Testament in vain when looking for promises of land restoration for the Jews. If such a restoration were to be expected, surely the whole New Testament would not be silent. Christ often predicted the fall of national Israel but never of a land restoration in Palestine. Christ implies that a national restoration of Israel as His chosen people should not be expected (Matt. 21:19,43-45). When He said "Let no fruit grow on thee henceforward for ever" (Matt. 21:19), He was using a fig tree to symbolize national Israel. Christ never offered any land hope to Israel, and neither does any New Testament writer.

There is a good reason for this New Testament silence. Israel's only hope was in and through Christ and His church. It was not a land but a salvation hope. Salvation was on an individual, not a national basis, and it would be obtained in the same way for Jews and Gentiles alike. There are no definite New Testament statements concerning the present state of Israel, and none should be read into it. Israel's future is exactly like that of every other nation; God has no chosen nation as such today. As has been shown earlier, the church has replaced Israel as God's chosen; the church, however, knows no national boundaries. The present hope of Jews is Christ, not land, and the same can be said for every nationality on earth.

Chapter Summary

Concerning Israel in prophesy, what are the facts? From now to eternity the Christian church, not Israel, is God's chosen. Israel as a nation rejected her promised Messiah and can be elected only individually. God's purpose is to redeem any (Jew or Gentile) who will submit to Christ. He does not have a secondary plan; it is either accept Christ or be lost.

Israel's present status is not due to any unfilled prophecy. It resulted from gift and conquest, and she may yet possess all of Palestine by this method. Contrary to many modern prophets, the future of Israel is unknown. According to the Book of Hebrews, the whole Jewish system with its Temple, priesthood, sacrifices, etc., served its purpose and passed away long ago. It was replaced with something far better, something eternal and universal in nature. God will never again need a pictorial sacrificial system, a special plot of land, or a special people. The cross is a guarantee that this will forever be true.

Chapter 5

Prophecy and Daniel's Seventy Weeks

Future events do not necessitate this chapter because Daniel's 70 weeks are now history. Many erroneous claims, however, do demand a response. Much of dispensational futuristic theology is derived from Daniel 9 or assumptions concerning Daniel 9. This chapter is considered by dispensationalists to be the very backbone of prophecy. Daniel 9 should be read at this point in its entirety; nevertheless, our primary purpose is to deal with the 70 weeks.

The Setting:

Daniel 9:1-23

As Daniel 9 begins, the captive-Daniel-is pictured as understanding from Jeremiah 25:11,12, and 29:10 that the Babylonian captivity should be near its end. Daniel understood it was to last 70 consecutive years.

He evidently saw no indication of a plan to release the Jews and therefore indicated that he thought the promised release might be conditional. At any rate he was praying and confessing both his sins and the sins of the Jewish people when the angel – Gabriel – touched him and said "…O Daniel, I am now come forth to give thee skill and understanding" (Dan. 9:22). Notice that Daniel is supposed to be able to UNDERSTAND the vision of 70 weeks which

Gabriel gave him. While Daniel was praying about a physical release, the vision he received included a Messiah who would provide for spiritual release from the captivity of sin. The Messiah would do this near the end of a specified block of time herein called 70 weeks.

Before getting into the vision itself, it should be understood that this passage of Scripture is interpreted in a great variety of ways. This is not, however, as important as it might at first seem. The most important thing is not the great variety of ways in which the weeks are said to be fulfilled; the real issue is whether or not the weeks are fulfilled. This does make a tremendous difference. Premillennialists say the 70 weeks are not fulfilled, while all other say they are. There is actually no specific postmillennial or amillennial view as far as the starting and ending of the weeks are concerned. They may hold the same or differing views on this, but both agree on the real issue, and that is that the 70 weeks are now history. We thus have a postmillennial and amillennial view of the 70 weeks being a fulfilled block of time versus a premillennial or futuristic view of an unfulfilled block of time. Daniel obviously did not teach both views; therefore, his vision must be carefully analyzed.

The Time and Purpose:

Daniel 9:24

The purpose of the 70 weeks is at least partially revealed in Daniel 9:24. It says:

Seventy weeks are determined upon thy people and upon thy holy city, to finish the transgression, and to make an end of sins, and to make reconciliation for iniquity, and to bring in everlasting righteousness, and to seal up the vision and prophecy, and to anoint the most Holy.

The premillennial view holds that most or all of these six things are yet to be accomplished, and therefore, the 70 weeks cannot now be fulfilled. There are variations in both the futuristic and fulfilled views, but they will now be presented jointly.

1. "To finish the transgression." Some futurists believe this will be done when God brings an end to Israel's rebellion during a future tribulation period (Daniel's 70th week), while others maintain it will happen afterward during an expected earthly millennium.

Some who present the fulfilled view say it refers to the finished work of Christ on Calvary; He finished transgression in the sense that He became sin for us (2 Cor. 5:21; Isa. 53:5). It is believed that no animal sacrifice will ever again suffice (Heb. 7:24-28; 9:11-15,26). A second view is that it refers to the Jews crowning their transgression with the act of rejecting and crucifying their Messiah. This does not mean that Jews would never sin again individually. It is looked upon as their last act as a nation before being rejected by God. They would soon pass away nationally and be replaced by the church. In other words, it was the act of crucifying Christ that brought national rejection to Israel and hope to the church – Jew or Gentile. Both fulfilled views point to the crucifixion.

2. "To make an end of sins." The first futurist view is that this expression refers to something that will take place during a future tribulation period; that is, God will at that time forgive repentant Jews of their sins. The second futuristic view is that the expression refers to a time following a tribulation period and the return of Christ when God will bring final judgment upon some Jews.

The fulfilled view is that Christ paid for sin when He was crucified. When John introduced Christ, he said,

"Behold the Lamb of God, which taketh away sin of the world" (Jn. 1:29). Again the Bible says, "...But now once in the end of the world hath he appeared to put away sin by the sacrifice of himself" (Heb. 9:26). The sacrifice of Christ on the cross legally ended all other sacrifices. Since the Temple was not immediately destroyed, sacrifices might temporarily still be made, but they would accomplish nothing; Heaven would never again recognize them. There would have been no purpose for the cross if animal sacrifices could still be recognized as valid. The fulfilled view is that sin was paid for by Christ and no other payment will be accepted even if it is offered by a Jew.

3. "To make reconciliation for iniquity." Premillennialists present two interpretations for the meaning of this expression. The first is that it can only refer to a Jewish reconciliation during a future tribulation period, a time when many Jews are expected to be converted to Christ. This is at least a consistent interpretation. The second view is that Christ made reconciliation for iniquity when He was crucified. This means that on one of the six issues this second group of premillennialists depart from the futuristic interpretation. This, we think, is correct, but for them it is inconsistent. Daniel was revealing what would happen in the 70 prophetic weeks, but both of these groups hold that Christ was crucified in a gap time period outside of the 70 weeks.

The fulfilled view is consistent and maintains that Christ made the "reconciliation for iniquity" through His crucifixion. The Bible supports this view when it declares, "And, having made peace through the blood of his cross, by him to RECONCILE all things unto himself..." (Col. 1:20). Again it says, "For if, when we were enemies, we were RECONCILED to God by the death of his Son, much more, being RECONCILED, we shall be saved by his life" (Rom. 5:10). (See also Heb. 2:17; Eph. 2:16; 2 Cor. 5:19; Tit. 2:14.)

4. "To bring in everlasting righteousness." Premillennialists say this will not happen until Christ returns and sets up his millennial reign. Again this is inconsistent because it is outside of Daniel's 70 weeks.

The fulfilled view is that Christ did this by redeeming us at Calvary. God's Word says, "But now the RIGHTEOUSNESS of God without the law is manifested....Even the RIGHTEOUSNESS of God which is by faith of Jesus Christ...to declare his RIGHTEOUSNESS for the remission of sins..." (Rom. 3:21, 22,25). (See also Heb. 9:12; 1 Pet. 2:24; 2 Cor. 5:21; Rom. 10:24.) When speaking of these accomplishments, George Murray affirmed: "How sickening it must be to many of the Lord's people, how subversive of truth and how insulting to the Lord Himself to insist that this has not yet happened, but is still in the future."[1]

5. "To seal up the vision and prophecy." Most often premillennialists do not attempt to put a specific time upon this fifth predicted accomplishment. They believe it refers to some point in history when God will terminate his dealing directly with the Jews through dreams, visions, angelic appearances, etc. because these will no longer be necessary.

The fulfilled view is that this too was accomplished by Christ. He was the fulfillment of the Old Testament prophecy which had often been revealed through visions. There are basically two views concerning how Christ did this. The first view says the "seal" is similar to an official notarized seal on a document. The official seal is the sign of approval and authority. Christ sealed Old Testament prophecy through His crucifixion by completing or fulfilling its shadows. The other fulfilled view sees the main idea as something being sealed up out of sight so it will not appear anymore; its purpose is fulfilled. Therefore, all Old Testament prophecy of a coming Messiah is now finished or sealed; it is history. The Old Testament prophetic system was closed or sealed by Christ the Messiah. Either fulfilled view gives Christ credit for sealing up visions and prophecy.

6. "And to anoint the most Holy." Because of a greater amount of difficulty surrounding this sixth predicted purpose, there are a greater variety of interpretations. Four primary premillennial explanations are: 1) It refers to a future anointing of a Millennial Temple, 2) it refers to the cleansing of the Second Temple of Judas Maccabeus in 165 B.C., 3) it refers to the anointing of the Heavenly Temple or New Jerusalem, or 4) it refers to the cleansing of a Jewish temple during Daniel's 70th week or tribulation period.

The fulfilled view also has a great variety of explanations. One thing we know for sure is that some place, person, or people were to be "anointed" during Daniel's 70 weeks. Explanations include: 1) If it refers to a place, it could have been fulfilled when Judas Maccabeus cleansed the Temple in 165 B.C., or it could refer to Jesus cleansing the Temple (Matt. 21:12,13; Mk. 11:12-21; Lk. 19:45,46). 2) It could have found its fulfillment when God's New Testament temple or dwelling place (Christians) was anointed with the Holy Ghost at Pentecost (Acts 2:1-4). 3) A third fulfilled view is that it refers to the anointing of the Holy one- Jesus. The Hebrew word *godesh* is here translated "holy" and can refer to a person as well as a place. Christ was anointed at His baptism (Matt. 3:13-17; Mk. 1:9-11; Lk. 3:21,22). (See also Acts 4:27; 10:28.) It seems most logical that Christ was the most Holy who was anointed, but either of these fulfilled views fit within Daniel's 70 weeks.

We thus have two very opposite views of how the six purposes of Daniel 9:24 were to be fulfilled. The premillennial view almost completely ignores the fact that Christ accomplished these things; it places them off into the future. The postmillennial and amillennial views give Christ credit for their fulfillment through His crucifixion.

The Time Pattern:

Daniel 9:25,26a

Daniel 9:25,26 present the pattern of Daniel's 70 weeks that were introduced in verse 24. The 70 weeks were passed over there so they could be dealt with here along with the pattern. The Hebrew word *shabua* which is here translated into English as "week" does not necessarily mean a week of days. It is an indefinite period of time; it could be a second, a minute, an hour, a day, a month, or a year. The word *shabua* is literally a seven or heptad, but not necessarily of days or weeks. Therefore, Daniel spoke literally of 70 sevens and not necessarily of 70 weeks.

It is not surprising, due to the uncertainty of the language, that the pattern of Daniel's 70 weeks is interpreted in a variety of ways. It should be remembered, however, that the most important thing is not the particular pattern into which these weeks are divided, but the important issue is whether or not the 70 (prophetic) weeks are presently fulfilled. This is the real issue that shapes theological opinions. Nevertheless, we will discuss the main patterns used to divide up Daniel's 70 weeks of years.

1. The Liberal Pattern. This view is that the 70 weeks are simply a block of prophetic time that ended with the rule of Antiochus Epiphanes and his defeat by the Maccabees. The "Messiah the Prince" of the passage is not believed to refer to Christ but to the high priest, Onias III, who was killed by Antiochus. This seems untenable.

2. The Traditional Pattern. This view is that 70 weeks are symbolic of a block of time beginning with the edict of Cyrus in 536 or 538 B.C. and ending with the

destruction of Jerusalem and the Temple in A.D. 70. All events are, therefore, limited to the first advent of Christ, especially to His being crucified. The 70 weeks, a block of prophetic time, are fulfilled. Since the years are symbolical rather than chronological, they do not have to total exactly 490. These exponents do not agree with the widely held view that Daniel's 70sevens are literally 70 x 7 or 490 years (not weeks). Some credit Augustine with originating this traditional view. That may be questionable because a number of others have expounded basically the same view.

3. John Calvin's Pattern. This view is basically the same as the traditional pattern just presented except it ends the prophetic block of time approximately three years after the Messiah is crucified rather than extending it to A.D. 70. The 69th week of time ended at Christ's baptism, and the 70th week started immediately thereafter with the earthly ministry of Christ. Accordingly, the Messiah is cut off or crucified in the middle of the 70th week; the latter half of the 70th week followed the crucifixion and was a time when the gospel was still presented to the Jews exclusively. The time period of the last half of the 70th week extended from the crucifixion through the historical events of the first nine chapters of Acts. Then the gospel was opened to the Gentiles, first by Peter and then by others. Actually Calvin is only one among many who hold this view.

4. The Dispensational Pattern. This view is that the 70 sevens of Daniel equal 490 years since 70 x 7=490. Daniel 9:25 makes it rather plain that the 70 weeks begin with the "commandment to restore and to build Jerusalem," but there were four such decrees. They were: 1) the command of Cyprus in 536 or 538 B.C. (Ez. 1:2,3; Isa. 44:28), 2) the command of Darius in 519 or 520 B.C. (Ez. 6:1-18), 3) the command of Artaxerxes Longimanus in 457 B.C. (Ez. 7:1, 11-26), and 4) the command of Artaxerxes in 445 B.C. (Neh. 1 and 2).

One dispensational group chooses the decree of Artaxerxes in 445 B.C. and calculates that the 7 plus 62 sevens equals 69 sevens or 483 years which reaches to about A.D. 29, the year of the Messiah's death. However, this pattern does not use the crucifixion as the ending of the 69th week but another event of the same year. It holds that the 69th week or 483 years ended with Christ appearing in Jerusalem to present Himself as the Jewish Messiah riding upon the back of a donkey (Matt. 21:5; Zech. 9:9). He was at that time, however, rejected, and the 70th year did not begin. Accordingly, the 70th year is still future; it will be a seven-year future period known as the Great Tribulation Period.

Another dispensational group chooses the decree of Artaxerxes Longimanus in 457 or 454 B.C. and juggles the years so that the first 483 years end in the first part of A.D. 27, the time of Christ's baptism. This group ends the 69th week with Christ's baptism rather than His triumphal entry into Jerusalem near the time of His death. They agree with their dispensational brethren that the 69th week is not followed by the 70th week. The church age is a long gap of time that does not count. The 70th week is believed to be a tribulation period of the future.

5. The Non-Dispensational Literal View. Those holding this view start time with two different decrees. The first chooses the decree of Artaxerxes in about 457 B.C. What is calculated to be 483 years later (69 weeks), the "Messiah the Prince" of Daniel 9:25 is baptized and starts his ministry in A.D. 26. The 70th week of Daniel is believed to begin immediately, and three and one half years later in the middle of Daniel's 70th week the Messiah is cut off or crucified. During the last half of the week, the gospel was still presented exclusively to the Jews. Daniel's 70 weeks then became history.

A second group of this view thinks the time must start with Cyrus who gave his edict in about 536 B.C. While others often claim this edict was only to rebuild the Temple and not the city, this group quickly points out that this is not true according to Isaiah. He said, "That saith of Cyrus, He is my shepherd, and shall perform all my pleasure: even saying to JERUSALEM, Thou shalt be built; and to the temple, Thy foundation shall be laid" (Isa. 44:28). By juggling figures, however, these can also come out with the 69th week ending with Christ baptism. The 70th week follows immediately with the crucifixion in the middle of it. After about three and one half more years during which the gospel was proclaimed exclusively to the Jews, Daniel's 70 weeks became history.

The preceding five views are certainly not exhaustive; there are other variations. How can groups start with different dates and end up at the same date? First, we are not told how long a year was or what calendar was to be used. A Jewish year was 354 days, a prophetic year 360 days, and a solar year was 365 and one fourth days. Over a period of 490 years this can make a significant difference.

Second, some adjust for about a four or five year mistake Dionysius made in the Christian calendar while other do not. Those who adjust have Christ's birth dated at about 4 B.C. and His crucifixion about A.D. 29. Those who make no adjustment in the Christian calendar do not agree on exactly how much it should be adjusted.

Third, a number of interpreters look upon the weeks or years as symbolic, not chronological. They can, for example, say that Daniel's 70 weeks began with Cyrus in about 536 B.C. and ended with the destruction of Jerusalem in A.D. 70. This is, of course, more than 490 chronological years, but that is not thought of as being important.

In spite of variations of interpretation, what is the chief message of Daniel 9:25,26a? It states:

Know therefore and understand, that from the going forth of the commandment to restore and to build Jerusalem unto the Messiah the Prince shall be seven weeks, and threescore and two weeks: the streets shall be built again, and the wall, even in troublous times. And after threescore and two weeks shall Messiah be cut off, but not for himself...

The starting point for the block of time is said to begin with "the commandment to restore and to build Jerusalem." From this commandment "UNTO the Messiah" is 69 of Daniel's 70 weeks. This is generally believed to mean unto His baptism, occasionally unto His triumphant entry into Jerusalem, but never unto His birth. This is only a difference of about three and one half years on the first 69 weeks of Daniel's vision.

It is important to notice that after this "UNTO" we have to be in the 70th week for it is plainly revealed that the 69th week expired with the "UNTO the Messiah." There is absolutely no Scripture, no logic, or reason to claim that the weeks are not consecutive. A gap to divide the 69th and 70th weeks is absurd; none of the other weeks are divided. We are told that neither Daniel nor any Old Testament character understood this gap or church age. How different from what the Bible itself says! Gabriel told Daniel he was bringing him "skill and understanding" (v. 22) and again in verse 23 he is told to "understand."

Could Daniel or anyone else understand such a gap? This gap is sometimes likened unto a yardstick with the last inch cut off and reattached with a super elastic that could be stretched a great distance. Even if this were possible it would not be 36 inches anymore and could not be used as a yardstick.

A gap can also be likened unto a foreigner entering the United States at Los Angeles who has no understanding of geography. That foreigner knows that he wants to go to Chicago and inquires about how to do so. He is told to travel eastward for 70 miles, and he does so, but there is no Chicago. He inquires and is told by another person that there was a gap of some 2,000 miles of which he was not informed. Would it not be cruel to give such an explanation to a stranger? Yet, it is even worse to claim God's Word uses such a method and divides Daniel's 69th and 70th weeks by what is already nearly 2,000.

Contracts would be absolutely useless if people were allowed to insert gaps. A highway contractor might bid to build a strip of road in New York and later be told by someone who inserted a gap that he would have to go to California to finish the project. When a building is contracted to be built in a certain number of days, the builder cannot insert a 2,000 year gap. When a note is due at the bank, the borrower cannot insert a gap of time. Surely human government is not superior to God!

According to the Biblical account itself, 69 weeks brings us "UNTO the Messiah." What happens then? "And AFTER threescore and two weeks shall Messiah be cut off..." (Dan. 9:26). This clearly means AFTER 62 weeks in addition to the 7 weeks mentioned in the previous verse, that is, AFTER the 69 weeks the Messiah would be crucified. AFTER cannot mean during or within; it means following. What week follows the 69th week? There is not but one week that can follow the 69th week and that is the 70th week. To claim that Christ was crucified, not during Daniel's 70th week but during a gap when time did not count, is unbelievable. Neither Gabriel nor Daniel hinted at any such reasoning.

The Messiah or Prince?

Daniel 9:26b,27

This passage reads:

…and the people of the prince that shall come shall destroy the city and the sanctuary; and the end thereof shall be with a flood, and unto the end of the war desolations are determined. And he shall confirm the covenant with many for one week: and in the midst of the week he shall cause the sacrifice and the oblation to cease, and for the overspreading of abominations he shall make it desolate, even until the consummation, and that determined shall be poured upon the desolate.

The important question in Daniel 9:26b is who were the "people" and the "prince" predicted by Daniel to destroy Jerusalem and its Temple. The answer is that the "people of the prince" were the Romans and the "prince" was Titus. The people (Romans) under the prince (Titus) totally destroyed both Jerusalem and the Temple in A.D. 70. Whether or not this is considered as happening after or during the 70th week is secondary. The important thing is that it is now history. How amazing that some would push this off into the future and claim that a new Roman Empire and Prince are coming! It is all supposed to be recorded here in Daniel 9.

Verse 27 continues, "And he shall confirm the covenant with many for one week." Who is the "he" the Messiah or the prince referred to in the previous verse? Again some make it future by saying the "he" is the prince and take this prince not to be Titus, but a future antichrist who will make a covenant with Israel during what they call the Great Tribulation Period. They further state that in the middle of Daniel's 70th week (the tribulation period), he (antichrist) will break the covenant and stop allowing the

Jewish sacrifices to be made. This interpretation should be rejected for a number of reasons.

The "he" of verse 27 cannot refer to the prince. John L. Bray, a Southern Baptist writer, stated it well when he explained:

The "he " of verse 27 applies to the main subject of verse 26, which is the "Messiah," as it certainly cannot refer to the "people," nor can it refer to the "prince" because "he" is a pronoun referring to the previous subject and the "prince" is not the subject but the object of a modifying clause.[2]

This is a good point. A pronoun should not have as its antecedent the object of a modifying clause.

R. Bradley Jones also made a valid comment concerning the "he" of verse 27 when he said:

To make it refer back to the "prince" of verse 26, where that prince is not even the subject of the sentence, imposes upon the passage a foreign personage who has not been introduced by the prophet. Besides, it takes the action away from the purpose of the seventy sevens, as set forth in verse 24, and makes it the action of an imaginary Antichrist who continues the transgression, prolongs sin, denies reconciliation for iniquity, and brings in seven years of unrighteousness. In other words it contradicts and nullifies the whole meaning of the prophecy.[3]

For the sake of illustration let us suppose that the "he" could refer to the prince of the people. The people of the prince destroyed Jerusalem in A.D. 70, but dispensationalists tell us the Prince (antichrist) is yet to come. Ironside says:

A prince is in view who is yet to play a large part in prophecy. He, however, has not appeared yet, but the people, that is, the Roman people, were used as a scourge of God to punish Israel for their sins, and they destroyed Jerusalem and the Temple.[4]

This inconsistency separates the people of the prince from their prince by what is already about 1,900 years. The truth is that there is no antichrist in this verse.

The pronoun "he" can refer only to the noun "Messiah." So the Messiah is the one who confirmed the covenant with the Jews for one week, the 70th week of Daniel. Notice that the covenant was CONFIRMED, not made. It was already in existence but was confirmed by the Messiah in a special way for one prophetic week. How did Christ do this? It is general knowledge that His ministry to the Jews lasted about three and one half years before he was crucified. As explained previously, Christ continued His ministry though others exclusively to the Jews for another three and one half years. Then Peter opened the door to the Gentiles (Acts 10). This is clearly Daniel's 70th week.

It is stated that the Messiah would confirm the covenant with "MANY" for one week. How many? John answers by saying, "He came unto his own, and his own received him not. But AS MANY as received him, to them gave he power to become the sons of God, even to them that believe on his name" (Jn. 1:11,12). Also when Christ instituted the Lord's Supper He spoke of the testament or covenant as a new one. (See also Heb. 8:6-13; 12:24; 13:20.)

But notice what else the Messiah did. The Bible says, "...And in the midst of the week he shall cause the sacrifice and the oblation to cease..." (Dan. 9:27). Did Jesus fulfill this? Yes, by His crucifixion in the middle of Daniel's 70th week, He put a legal end to the Jewish sacrificial system. He was the Lamb of God that was sacrificed once and for all for the sins of the world. He fulfilled and abolished the shadowy Mosaic system. When Christ cried out on the cross, "It is finished," this at least included the Jewish system of animal sacrifices. It is true that Christ allowed the Temple to stand a few more years, but the need for sacrifices was finished and in time the Temple was also. Any attempt of animal sacrifices for sin beyond the cross is degrading to the Messiah who bore those sins in His own body. Praise God, a sufficient atonement was made by Christ and no animal sacrifice can atone.

The last part of verse 27 is somewhat awkward in the English translation, but it is simply a prediction of the soon coming end to Jerusalem and the Temple. This harmonizes with Christ's own prediction (Matt. 23:37,38; 24:1,2). We now know that it became a historical fact in A.D. 70 (Lk. 21:20).

But what difference does it make whether or not one believes Daniel's 70 weeks are fulfilled or unfulfilled? Look at the great contrast of the two opposite views. 1) The unfulfilled view says there is a big gap between the 69th and the 70th weeks, while the fulfilled view says the weeks follow each other in logical sequence. 2) The unfulfilled view credits a future antichrist for ending animal sacrifices, while the fulfilled view credits Christ with making an atonement which left animal sacrifices unnecessary. 3) The unfulfilled view has an antichrist making and breaking a future covenant with the Jews, while the fulfilled view has the Messiah confirming (not making and breaking) a covenant with the Jews during His first advent. 4) The unfulfilled view places great significance upon a future antichrist, while the fulfilled view presents the Messiah as the grand theme of Daniel 9. 5) The unfulfilled view says the expression "to finish the transgression" is something that is yet to happen, while the fulfilled view is that it happened when Christ was crucified. 6) The unfulfilled view says that the expression "to make and end of sins" refers to God's pardoning the Jews either during or after a future tribulation period, while the fulfilled view says this happened when Christ was crucified. 7) The unfulfilled view says "to bring in everlasting righteousness" will not happen until what they call the millennium, while the fulfilled view is that Christ accomplished this at His first advent through His crucifixion.

Chapter Summery

What is the truth concerning Daniel's 70 weeks? The truth is that Daniel's 70 weeks are now history. The Messiah the Prince, of whom Daniel spoke, has already fulfilled the things He was predicted to accomplish. We should give Christ and Calvary proper credit. Never should one allow a so-called future Roman antichrist to strip Christ of His honor.

Nevertheless, dispensationalists assure us that God still has a separate program and destiny for Israel and the church; that there is a future seven-year tribulation period which is Daniel's 70th week; that there is a future Roman antichrist; and that the whole church age is a gap between Daniel's 69th and 70th weeks. It is all said to be found in Daniel 9, the so-called backbone of prophecy. To non-dispensationalists this is unbelievable.

Chapter 6

Prophecy and Antichrists

Opinions concerning antichrists vary not only among the three broad views of premillennialism, post-millennialism, and amillennialism, but also within each group. Some place great emphasis upon the subject of antichrist in spite of obvious uncertainties. All premillennialists, many amillennialists, and a few postmillennialists think there will be a personal antichrist who will appear a short time before the Second Coming of Christ. There is absolutely no agreement on who he was or shall be. Some from among both amillennialists and postmillennialists do not believe the Bible teaches that there is to be one personal antichrist of the future. They maintain that there have been many antichrists in the past and more will continue to appear.

In spite of all that is said and written on the subject, the word "antichrist" or "antichrists" only appears in four verses of the Bible. The word is not capitalized in most Bibles. This writer uses mainly the King James Version, and antichrist is never capitalized in it. Evidently the translators did not think it should be made to refer to a particular person. Several other translations have been checked and the results are the same. However, religious literature is filled with examples of antichrist being capitalized.

What man says has little value, but what the Bible states concerning antichrists is of utmost importance. The only four verses which mention antichrists are as follows:

Little children, it is the last time: and as ye have heard that antichrist shall come, even now are there many antichrists; whereby we know that it is the last time (1 Jn. 2:18).

Who is a liar but he that denieth that Jesus is the Christ? He is antichrist, that denieth the Father and the Son (1 Jn. 2:22).

And every spirit that confesseth not that Jesus Christ is come in the flesh is not of God: and this is that spirit of antichrist, whereof ye have heard that it should come; even now already is it in the world (1 Jn. 4:3).

For many deceivers are entered into the world, who confess not that Jesus Christ is come in the flesh. This is a deceiver and an antichrist (2 Jn. 7).

The foregoing verses give the total Biblical message on the word antichrist. John alone uses the word so it is important to understand how he used it. He also wrote the Book of Revelation and spoke of a "beast" and a "false prophet," but never called either of them an antichrist. By a dictionary definition this beast or false prophet might be an antichrist, but John, the writer, did not say so. Paul spoke of a "man of sin," but he never called him an (the) antichrist. How then did John use the word antichrist?

In 1 John 2:18, John reminded his readers that they were already living in the "last time" or last days. The whole church age is the time of the last covenant, or last days (Acts 2:17). John did not paint a picture of one great antichrist who would be destroyed by Christ at His Second Coming. Many, however, think that Paul by inference did (2 Thess. 2:3-8). Let it be admitted, however that the word antichrist is not used that way by John. John further reminded his readers that they had previously been taught that "antichrist shall come" and "many antichrists" had already done so at the time he was writing (1 Jn. 2:18). First John 2:18 establishes the fact that antichrists were already a reality in a variety of persons. This verse does not, however, define what an antichrist is.

The next passage (1 Jn. 2:22) supplements what John had just said by defining antichrist. It was a person who "denies that Jesus is the Christ" or Messiah. It is not enough to claim God as one's Father. To do so and not acknowledge Christ as the divine Messiah, Son of God, and Savior is "antichrist." One cannot have the Father apart from the Son; God has made only one plan of redemption, and that was by the sacrifice of His Son. John taught that those who did not believe this were antichrists. That is clearly how John used this word which no other Bible writer used. John did not say one had to claim to be Christ or Messiah in order to be antichrist. Others by inference may teach this, but John did not.

John could have been talking about people of his day who did not consider Christ a total impostor, but who simply wore His name without giving it full honors. These antichrists were referred to as persons who had gone "out from us, but they were not of us…" (1 Jn. 2:19). They were religious people who became antichrists. They may have thought of Christ as a great person, but only as a man. For some reason they tried to attach themselves to Christian groups, an attachment which led to trouble.

The deity of Christ is so important to Christianity that it must be defended at all cost. The antichrists that John knew were religious persons rather than atheists, infidels, or heathens.

The third passage (1 Jn. 4:3) refers to some group or groups who would not confess "that Jesus Christ is come in the flesh," and they are said to possess a "spirit of antichrist." This verse could have had reference to Gnostics of John's day who questioned the reality of the human side of Christ. They seemed to have believed in a heavenly Christ but not in an incarnate one. There were also Docetists in John's day who taught that the body of Christ was a mere phantom, not flesh. The antichrists were professed Christians whose doctrines caused them to be classified by John as persons who had the spirit of antichrist.

The fourth passage (2 Jn. 7) is basically repetition of what John had earlier said (1 Jn. 4:3). It therefore referred to Gnostics, Docetists, or other false religious teachers.

This is everything that the Bible says about the word "antichrist." It may be summarized as follows:

1. Many antichrists already existed at the time John wrote about them. The word antichrist in the Bible does not refer simply to one great end-time ruler.

2. The antichrists John wrote about were not atheists, infidels, heathens, supernatural supermen, resurrected persons, Satan incarnated, beasts, or political rulers such as Nero, Mussolini, Hitler, etc.

3. The antichrists John spoke of were professed Christians who taught false doctrines that degraded Christ. They did not believe He was both truly human and divine.

4. The antichrist John spoke of were not said to be types or forerunners of one great-end time antichrist; that may be, but John did not say they were.

5. The antichrists John spoke of were religious deceivers, but not impersonators.

6. Not a single reference in Daniel, Ezekiel, Matthew, 2 Thessalonians, or Revelation speaks of an antichrist that can be Biblically connected to the four verses in John which speak of antichrists. Any attempt to connect other Scriptures with 1 and 2 John is pure inference.

The dispensational antichrist might make interesting fiction, but is he Scriptural? The dispensational end-time antichrist gives the verses in John a meaning far different from their initial intent. Those who see a connection between the "antichrists" of John and the "beast" of Revelation might need to remember that the author of those two works (John) failed to make any such connection.

In spite of the foregoing conclusion, a connection by inference is frequently made between other Scriptural passages and those in John. Let us examine them.

Daniel's Little Horn – Daniel 7:8

Daniel had a vision of four beasts; each of which represented some kingdom that was future at the time of the vision. The fourth beast represented the Roman Empire, and its ten horns were ten different kings or emperors of the Kingdom. There also arose another leader in the Roman kingdom which was pictured in the vision as a "little horn." Daniel says, "I considered the horns, an, behold, there came up among them another little horn, before whom there were three of the firsts horns plucked up by the roots…" (Dan. 7:8).

Daniel spoke of the rise of some person out of the Roman Empire and then told of a number of actions he would take. He did not name the person, and people can only speculate as to who he was or will be. The most frequent interpretation is that Daniel's prophecy was fulfilled by Antiochus Epiphanes. Others, however, think it was fulfilled by Julius Caesar, Vespasian, Titus, the papacy, etc.

Some think Antiochus Epiphanes fulfilled the prophecy, but not completely. These maintain there will be a second and more complete fulfillment in an antichrist of the yet future, an antichrist that will be destroyed by Christ at His Second Coming. Of course, this means that the old Roman Empire will have to be established again in the future.

It should be understood that such an antichrist would be different from John's antichrist; John never used the word antichrist to refer to a world ruler. Furthermore, the building of a doctrine upon a possible second fulfillment of a prophecy is highly questionable. We do not deny the possibility of a prophecy having a second fulfillment, but maintain that it is risky as a method of establishing doctrine.

People often speak of a great end-time antichrist rising up out of a revived Roman Empire as something yet to happen because Daniel said it would. That is only an assumption. Whether this prophecy is presently fulfilled or unfulfilled is a matter of interpretation.

Daniel's Abomination of Desolation

Daniel 9:27; Matthew 24:15; Luke 21:20

And he shall confirm the covenant with many for one week: and in the midst of the week he shall cause the sacrifice and the oblation to cease, and for the overspreading of abominations he shall make it desolate even until the consummation, and that determined shall be poured upon the desolate (Dan. 9:27).

When ye therefore shall see the abomination of desolation, spoken of by Daniel the prophet, stand in the holy place, (whoso readeth, let him understand) (Matt. 24:15).

And when ye shall see Jerusalem compassed with armies, then know that the desolation thereof is nigh (Lk. 21:20).

Some say that the "prince" of Daniel 9:27 is a yet future antichrist who will be an abomination and desolator by desecrating a Jewish Temple that is also yet to be built. It is all said to be plainly established by Daniel's prophecy. Of course, this is only one interpretation.

To avoid repetition the reader is encouraged to read chapter 5 from this book.

Matthew does plainly speak of "the abomination of desolation, spoken of by Daniel the prophet." It is generally agreed that Matthew's "holy place," however, was the Jewish Temple of his day, the Temple that the discussion of Matthew 24 was about. He did not refer to some yet future Temple even though one may be built. Jesus would not likely refer to such a future Temple with its reinstatement of animal sacrifices as a holy place. It certainly would not be in accord with the Biblical Book of Hebrews which pictures animal sacrifices as presently useless.

Matthew does not interpret who or what the abomination of desolation spoken of by Daniel was. He did not indicate that he was referring to an end-time person. How then do we know to whom Matthew was referring?

When reporting on the Olivet prophecy, Luke did let us know who the abomination of desolation was. He said, "And when ye shall see Jerusalem compassed with armies, then know that the desolation thereof is nigh." (Lk. 21:20). By reading the surrounding verses one cannot deny that this is a parallel account to Matthew's Olivet Discourse found in chapter 24. Parallel accounts cannot have a different meaning. By combining Luke's statement with secular history it is clear that Titus and his Roman army were the abomination of desolation. It was fulfilled in A.D. 70 when the Romans desecrated and destroyed the Temple and Jerusalem. Matthew 24:15 and Luke 21:20 are parallel accounts speaking of the same event.

Those who believe in a future end-time antichrist generally agree that Titus and his army were a fulfillment of the abomination of desolation but insist that it will have a greater future fulfillment. What shall we say then? We are back to building a doctrine of a future antichrist on a possible, but not probable, second fulfillment of prophecy.

The Beast or Beasts of Revelation

Revelation 13

The reader is encouraged to read Revelation 13 at this time. The first beast (13:1-10, 18) rises up out of the sea and is often thought of as a future antichrist. Futurists, especially dispensational futurists, think this beast is yet to come. They claim (without proof) that everything in Revelation 4-19 will happen in a future seven-year tribulation period, a period that is Daniel's 70th week. We have already shown that Daniel's 70 weeks are all history. There are several methods of interpreting Revelation; the futurist method is just one.

One traditional interpretation holds that the beast was Nero, whose name numerically equals 666 (v. 18), while others believe it was Nero's personality reincarnated in the person of Domitian. By making one of the Roman emperors the "beast," Revelation is made relevant to the people for whom it was written (Rev. 1:1-3).

Many time clocks are made with Roman numerals, but since the numerals equal numbers, one can tell time by them. In the Aramaic language (the language of John's day), Nero Caesar was NRONKSR. The Aramaic numerical values are:

N =	50
R =	200
O =	6
N =	50
K=	100
S =	60
R =	200
Total =	666

In the Hebrew language Nero Caesar is NERONKESAR and also has a numerical value of 666.

Some Protestant writers believe that the papacy or Roman Church is the beast. The title of the pope in Latin is VICARIUSFILII DEI which in English means Vicar of the Son of God. This title of the pope also has a numerical value of 666.

V=	5
I=	1
C=	100
A=	0
R=	0
I=	1
U=	5
S=	0
F=	0
I=	1
L=	50
I=	1
I=	1
D=	500
E=	0
I=	1
Total=	666

It should be remembered, however, that viewing the papacy as the beast would have had little meaning to the people who lived between A.D. 65 and A.D. 95 because there was no papacy at that time.

A book could be written on the various views concerning the beast that rose up out of the sea. To build a doctrine about an end-time antichrist on a passage interpreted so many different ways is building a doctrine on a frail foundation. There could even be an example of a double reference in Revelation 13 with the beast being someone or something in the age the book was written but having a second fulfillment later. Speculation is, however, not an ideal way to establish doctrine.

The second beast of Revelation 13 rises up out of the earth (vv. 11-17) and is sometimes also pictured as a future antichrist. Those holding this view generally are futurists who believe the first beast to be a political antichrist and the second beast a religious antichrist. It is thought that they will rule together. A more common view among the futurists, however, is that the first beast will be the antichrist and the second beast will be his helper.

There are several traditional views. One is that the second beast was really a committee that tried to enforce emperor worship. Others think the second beast was the papacy who in time gained the protection of the Roman Empire. Some see the second beast as Jewish leaders who persecuted Christians. Naturally, this group believes that Revelation was written before Domitian. The possibilities are numerous for identifying this beast, but we will not take the time necessary to pursue further. The real question is, does it make sense to establish an elaborate doctrine on an apocalyptic passage that is not interpreted by the writer himself or any other Biblical writer? Surely wisdom dictates that more support is needed.

The Man of Sin

2 Thessalonians 2:3

We have now arrived at the strongest of all Biblical passages concerning the possibility of one great end-time antichrist, herein called "the man or sin." The passage reads as follows:

Now we beseech you, brethren, by the coming of our Lord Jesus Christ, and by our gathering together unto him, That ye be not soon shaken in mind, or be troubled, neither by sprit, nor by word, nor by letter as from us, as that day of Christ is at hand. Let no man deceive you by any means: for that day shall not come, except there come a falling away first, and the man of sin be revealed, the son of perdition; Who opposeth and exalteth himself above all that is called God, or that is worshipped; so that he as God sitteth in the Temple of God, shewing himself that he is God. Remember not, that, when I was yet with you, I told you these things? And now ye know what withholdest that he might be reveled in his time. For the mystery of iniquity doth already work: only he who now letteth will let, until he be taken out of the way. And then shall that Wicked be revealed, whom the Lord shall consume with the spirit of his mouth, and shall destroy with the brightness of his coming (2 Thess. 2:1-8).

There are three general interpretation of this passage. First, there is the fulfilled view which is held consistently, but not absolutely, by postmillennialists. Second, there is the futurist view which is held consistently by premillennialists although they do not agree on all detailed. Third, there is the view that it is past, present, and future, i.e., there already were antichrists in Paul's day, there are antichrists today, but there will yet be one great end-time antichrist. This is frequently the position of amillennialists. Of the three major views, the amillennialists (good or bad) are the least consistent when interpreting this passage.

Fulfilled View

The typical fulfilled view begins with the explanation that Paul was trying to help the people of Thessalonica with a problem that they had. Some had quit their jobs because they thought Christ had already come or that He would appear at any moment. Paul was thus dealing with a problem of that day, not some far off event. According to Paul, at least two events would have to happen before the Lord could return; there had to be a "falling away" (apostasy) and the revelation of the "man of sin."

The apostasy is sometimes thought to refer to what would soon happen in the Roman Catholic Church. The "man of sin" is thought to apply to the papacy. It is argued that the man of sin can refer to a succession of persons because Paul indicated that the man of sin existed at that time; he simply had not yet been revealed (vv. 5-8). Paul further stated that this person would be destroyed by Christ at His coming (v.8). The point is that a succession of persons must be referred to for no individual would live that long, a time period already nearly 2,000 years in length.

Those of the fulfilled view are not sure who the restrainer was (vv. 6,7) but generally believe he was connected to the Roman government in some way. It is emphasized that neither the Holy Spirit nor the church was the restrainer (a popular futurist concept) because Paul would not have been afraid to name the Holy Spirit or the church. They further emphasize that there is no hint in the passage of a rapture of the church or a departure of the Holy Spirit from this world. It is believed that Paul's readers already knew the identity of the restrainer (v. 6) thus making it unnecessary for Paul to name him. This, however, left modern readers without the answer; they can only speculate.

A few postmillennialists present a different fulfilled view. They believe that since Paul wrote this passage about A.D. 54 and the Lord did not bring the Jewish nation to an end until A.D. 70, the apostasy or fall referred to in the passage was a Jewish apostasy. Therefore, Paul referred to the real Temple of Jerusalem (v.5), not a building or church related to a pope. The man of sin did not refer to a succession of popes but to Roman emperors who frequently demanded worship. This group maintains that Paul could have gotten his idea for the "man of sin" from the "abomination of desolation" Christ spoke of in his Olivet prophecy (Matt. 24:15; Lk. 21:20). If so, the prophecy was fulfilled in A.D. 70.

This latter group of postmillennialists does not believe the Second Coming of the Lord is referred to in verse 8. They think it was a coming of the Lord in judgment upon the Jews in A.D. 70. Examples of this type of coming may be found in Isaiah 19:1 and Micah 1:3. Most of those holding a fulfilled view (postmillennialists or amillennialists) believe, however, that when the expression "by the coming of our Lord Jesus Christ, and by our gathering together unto him" (V. 1) is considered alongside what is said in verse 8, it can only refer to the Second Coming of the Lord.

Futurist View

According to dispensationalists, the "falling away" or apostasy and the "man of sin" referred to in this passage are both end-time events. The "man of sin" will be a great end-time antichrist and will arise during a future seven-year tribulation period. This seven-year tribulation period is thought to be Daniel's 70th week of prophecy. These contend that this period is best described in Revelations 4-19; not here in 2 Thessalonians. Paul's "man of sin" is usually equated with Daniel's "little horn" and "abomination of desolation," and with the "beast" of revelations. They feel sure that the "man of sin" prophecy was not fulfilled in either the destruction of Jerusalem in A.D. 70 or by the papacy throughout history.

The futurist view usually maintains that the restrainer will be the Holy Spirit and the church through which he works. Both are to be removed from the world at what is called the rapture. This is not true, however, according to Posttribulation premillennialists or amillennialists, either of which may hold some type of futuristic view. While most futurists hold that the Holy Spirit is the restrainer, other opinions can be found.

All futurists, premillennialists or otherwise, believe that 2 Thessalonians 2:1,8 refer to the literal Second Coming of Christ and His personal destruction on the man of sin whether he be called antichrist or something else.

One serious problem the dispensational futurist is faced with in this passage is that Paul relates the whole story concerning the "man of sin" without any hint of a rapture of the church before the "man of sin" is revealed. When Paul gave two signs (apostasy and the "man of sin") that must be fulfilled before the Lord comes again, why did he not include a third (the rapture) and explain to the Thessalonians that they would be gone from the earth before the "man of sin" was revealed? If there is such a thing as a rapture of the church prior to the revelation of the "man of sin," Paul surely let an appropriate and opportune time pass without saying so.

Past, Present, and Future View

While some amillennialists basically agree with postmillennialists and hold the fulfilled view, the majority seem to hold the past, present, and future view. This group sees many fulfillments of apostasy and the "man of sin" in both the past and present. These, however, are looked upon as initial fulfillments and shadows of a greater end-time prophecy and antichrist. The last and greatest antichrist will be destroyed by Christ at His Second Coming. Paul's "man of sin" is taken as one of several names for the end-time antichrist.

What explanation do amillennialists give for being so uncertain concerning the "man of sin" and whether to believe in the fulfilled view or in the past, present, and future view? They seem to believe that it just does not pay to be dogmatic in naming the "man of sin". Most dogmatic persons have already been proven false prophets, and in time others will be also. Without exhausting the possibilities, those who have dogmatically been named as the great "man of sin" are: 1) an unnamed future atheistic superman, 2) the Jewish nation, 3) the Roman Empire, 4) a succession of Roman emperors, 5) Caligula, 6) Nero, 7) Nero raised from the dead in the future, 8) Judas Iscariot raised from the dead in the future, 9) Vespasian, 10) Titus, 11) Domitian, 12) Diocletian, 13) the little horn of Daniel, 14) Daniel's abomination of desolation, 15) the beast of Revelation, 16) the papacy, 17) Protestants, 18) Napoleon, 19) Kaiser Wilhelm, 20) Mussolini, 21) Hitler, 22) Stalin, 23) Kissinger (he even has sin in the middle of his name), 24) Mohammed, 25) Simon Magus, 26) Martin Luther and 27) Docetism or Gnosticism.

Amillennialists of the past, present, and future view are, therefore, slow to speculate on specifics while seeing many possible fulfillments in the process of history.

While a few amillennialists venture to express the view that the Holy Spirit is the restrainer, they are quick to point out that this does not mean they believe great numbers will be saved after the Holy Spirit is withdrawn. They do not believe in the concept of the 144,000 Jewish evangelists, without the convicting power of the Holy Spirit, leading the greatest revival in human history. Neither do they believe such revival is possible through a gospel of the kingdom minus the cross message; in other words, these amillennialists have no faith in a restored Judaism.

One group who speaks of the Holy Spirit as the restrainer, in contrast to dispensationalists who do so, believes that when the Holy Spirit is withdrawn, we will be in the "little season" period of Revelation 20, a time when Satan will be loosed. Accordingly, Satan of Revelation 20 is personified in Paul's "man of sin" and is defeated by Christ in the Battle of Armageddon (Rev. 16:9-21) or the Battle of Gog and Magog (Rev. 20:8,9). Unlike dispensationalists, amillennialists do not hold these to be two separate battles. These battles are simply a picture of Christ's victory over evil when He comes again.

Chapter Summary

The premillennial concept of connecting the antichrist of John with other Scriptural passages was well summarized by Boetther when he said:

Yet not one single reference in Daniel or Ezekiel or Paul or the Book of Revelation which Premillennialists allege refers to the Antichrist is connected in any way with the verses in the epistles of John that mention antichrist. All is based on inference. Let the reader search for himself and see how far-fetched that connection is. We make bold to say that this picture of Antichrist as a world ruler who persecutes the Jews during an alleged tribulation period and leads the armies of the Gentiles against the Jews in Palestine is pure fiction, without so much as one clear supporting verse in all Scriptures.[1]

In summary, the author has not named a particular antichrist or restrainer. It is doubtful that any present day individual can correctly do so; many are trying, however. Various views have been given, and the readers can make their own decision. Perhaps no decision should be made apart from the next chapter. A study of antichrists and tribulation actually cannot be separated.

Chapter 7

Prophecy and Tribulation

The subject of tribulation cannot be separated from the subject of antichrists. They have been placed in separate chapters only for convenience and clarity. All premillennialists, many amillennialists, and a few postmillennialists believe there will be a severe tribulation period shortly before the Second Coming of Christ. Dispensational premillennialists, however, place this tribulation period between what they call the rapture of the church and the revelation of Christ. In this case the rapture is not considered the Second Coming since Christ is said to only come in the air and not to the earth.

There is no general agreement about the exact length of this tribulation period by its various advocates. Some believe it will be three and one half years, others seven years, and still others will not speculate as to its length. Neither is there agreement on the purpose, nature, or events of the end-time tribulation.

Again, as in the case concerning antichrists, there are some who believe the great tribulation period (not all tribulation) is now past history. We therefore have the same three general interpretations of the tribulation period that we had concerning antichrists. First, there is the fulfilled view which is held consistently but not absolutely by postmillennialists. Second, there is the futurist view which is held consistently by premillennialists although there is no agreement on details. Third, there is the view that the tribulation period is past, present, and future. Accordingly, there has already been what the Bible refers to as the great tribulation period, but it was only an initial fulfillment; others are expected to follow. This is the position of most amillennialists; nevertheless, a good number of them accept the fulfilled view similar to postmillennialists.

The word "tribulation" or its equivalent is used many times in the Bible, but commentators generally use six or less of these as referring to an end-time tribulation period. These six passages are Jeremiah 30:7; Daniel 12:1; Matthew 24:21; Mark 13:19; Revelation 3:10; and Revelation 7:14. Two of these (Matt. 24and Mk 13) are generally taken to be parallel accounts of Christ's Olivet prophecy.

Jeremiah 30:7

Jeremiah says, "Alas! For that day is great, so that none is like it; it is even the time of Jacob's trouble; but he shall be saved out of it" (Jer. 30:7). The word tribulation is not in this particular passage, but all agree that it does predict tribulation by using the words "Jacob's trouble." In order to understand that to which Jeremiah referred, one should study the entire context of the passage. Even then different interpretations may occur.

Fulfilled View

Those of the fulfilled view, especially post-millennialists, emphasize that the Bible does not say that the time of Jacob's trouble is the same as either the great tribulation or Daniel's 70th week. They further maintain that there is no Biblical evidence that the time of Jacob's trouble is yet future. How then do they explain the passage?

Jeremiah prophesied before Nebuchadnezzar destroyed either Jerusalem or Solomon's Temple and prior to Judah's Babylonian captivity. The descendants of Jacob were warned that if they did not repent a time of trouble would come upon them. They failed to repent and suffered the consequences: 70 years of Babylonian captivity.

The latter part of Jeremiah 30:7 says "...But he (Jacob) shall be saved out of it." This was a promise that Jacob (Israel) would be delivered or permitted to return to their land. Did this happen? Yes, all who wanted to return to Judea did so under Zerubbabel, Ezra, or Nehemiah. They were given governmental assistance to return, construct another temple, and build a wall around their newly built city of Jerusalem. The time of Jacob's trouble referred to in Jeremiah 30:7 is therefore believed to be fulfilled, and not future.

Concerning this time of Jacob's trouble, Jeremiah prophesied that it would be such "...That none is like it..." (Jer. 30:7). Was this true of the events leading to and during the Babylonian captivity? Yes, in spite of many past losses, nothing up to that time equaled the destruction of Jerusalem with her beloved Temple. The Hebrew people had been in captivity before but had never left such precious memories behind.

Immediately following Jeremiah 30:7 the prophet starts promising deliverance. The promise continues not only to the end of chapter 30 but beyond. Jacob's trouble was predicted to last 70 years. Those of the fulfilled view are simply amazed that anyone would try to apply Jeremiah 30:7 to an end-time trouble and deliverance. Prophecies which have more than one fulfillment are believed to be accidental rather than by design. These see a great difference between Jeremiah's original intent and the intent of futurists who think the prophet was speaking of something even yet wholly future.

There is, however, a second fulfilled view that differs somewhat from this first type. Accordingly, it is believed that Jacob's trouble began with the Babylonian captivity but did not end with the return home. Jacob's trouble is believed to refer to all of Israel's trouble down through their whole history until, after rejecting Christ, they were nationally destroyed by the Romans in A.D. 70. It was, therefore, A.D. 70 before Jacob's trouble was completely fulfilled.

Futurist View

The dispensational futurist view is that "the time of Jacob's trouble" which Jeremiah referred to is the same as what they call the end-time great tribulation period and Daniel's 70th week. The future tribulation period is said to be seven years in length. The Bible nowhere says the tribulation period will last seven years, but it is built upon the supposition that the 70th week of Daniel's prophecy is yet future. Dispensationalists further say that the seven-year-tribulation period begins with the rapture of the church (another supposition) and concludes when the Lord returns. If this supposition were true, then everybody living during the seven-year tribulation period will know exactly the time of Christ's Second Coming. All that generation will need to do is count seven years from the date of the rapture and then look up. Any scheme that allows people to figure out when Jesus is coming has to be antibiblical and false. Without refuting again the supposition that Daniel's 70th week is future, the reader is encouraged to read again the chapter in this book on Daniel's Seventy weeks.

Obviously, all those who hold to the futurist view of Jacob's trouble are not dispensationalists. They do not connect future tribulation or trouble with Daniel's 70th week;

neither do they speculate on how long the trouble will last. They do, however, maintain that Jeremiah's prophecy refers to end-time trouble while not denying there may have been prior fulfillments. All premillennialists are futurists but not all futurists are premillennialists.

Past, Present and Future View

While many amillennialists agree with post-millennialists and hold the fulfilled view, others believe in the past, present, and future concept. They, therefore, generally believe that Jacob's trouble (Jer. 30:7) was fulfilled during the Babylonian captivity but not completely; other fulfillments would follow. Some amillennialists see in the words "Jacob's trouble" an initial fulfillment with Israel or Jews but foreshadowing a coming tribulation upon Christians (true Israel). These are tribulations in general, however, and only rarely are they connected to one end-time tribulation period. This does not necessarily deny an end-time tribulation; it simply finds little support for the idea from Jeremiah's prophecy.

Daniel 12:1

Daniel says:

And at that time shall Michael stand up, the great prince which standeth for the children of thy people: and there shall be a time of trouble, such as never was since there was a nation even to that same time: and at that time thy people shall be delivered, everyone that shall be found written in the book (Dan.12:1).

The obvious first step in interpreting this verse is the preceding chapter where a king is spoken of who defies God (Dan. 11:21, 36). The king, however, is not named, a fact that necessitates speculation.

The king referred to in Daniel 11:21, 36 and Daniel 12:1 is most often thought to be Antiochus Epiphanes, and the "time of trouble" was during his reign over the Jews in 171-165 B.C. This is also known as the Maccabean period. During this time Antiochus profaned the Temple by stopping the Jewish sacrifices, placing pagan sacrifices on the altar (including unclean swine), and by dedicating the Jewish Temple to the Greek god Zeus (1 Mac. 1:45,46,54; 2 Mac. 6:2). Antiochus was very cruel to the Jews causing them great tribulation.

The expression in Daniel 12:1 "…And at that time thy people shall be delivered…"is therefore interpreted as the Maccabean deliverance, the account of which is found in the books of Maccabees.

Others think that Daniel possibly was not referring to Antiochus Epiphanes but to Herod the Great, the papacy, or an end-time antichrist. The tying together of Daniel 12:1; Matthew 24:15; 2 Thessalonians 2:3; Revelations 13:1; etc. is nothing but speculation whether done by premillennialists, postmillennialists, or amillennialists. The passage is simply so vague or obscure that it should not be used to establish the doctrine of a particular end-time tribulation period.

Matthew 24

The Olivet Discourse of Matthew 24 is considered a major passage concerning a tribulation period. The reader should read Matthew 24 in its entirety. In this chapter, Jesus says, "For then shall be great tribulation, such as was not since the beginning of the world to this time, no, nor ever shall be" (Matt. 24:21). To what exactly was Jesus referring? We are back to our three broad views. First, there is the fulfilled view held consistently by postmillennialists. Second, there is the futurist view held consistently by premillennialists, nevertheless, these differ on details. Third, there is the past, present, and future view. Those of this view agree that there has already been great tribulation, there is presently great tribulation in some part of the world, but maintain that tribulation will continue and perhaps intensify during an end-time tribulation period. Most, but certainly not all, amillennialists hold to this third interpretation. Some basically agree with postmillennialists and follow the fulfilled view.

Fulfilled View

The previous chapter of Matthew closed with Christ predicting the fall of Jerusalem, and then saying, "Behold, your house is left unto you desolate" (Matt. 23:38). The disciples evidently wondered if Christ meant the great Temple, the house of God, which was the heart of the Jewish nation. They reminded Christ of the magnificent Temple buildings (Matt. 23:28). Jesus then said to them, "See ye not all these things? Verily I say unto you, There shall not be left here one stone upon another, that shall not be thrown down" (Matt. 24:2). They then decided he was talking about the Temple (not some future Temple) and asked further questions. They inquired, "...Tell us, when shall these things be? And what shall be the sign of thy coming, and of the end of the world?" (Matt. 24:3).

The first part of the question is clear enough. They want to know when the Temple will be destroyed. The next part of the question has caused a problem with interpretation. What did the disciples mean by "thy coming" and "end of the world"? Those of the fulfilled view do not believe these expressions refer to the yet Second Coming of Christ, and the burning of the world at the end-time. A number of reasons are given in support of this interpretation.

1) The disciples had no concept of the Second Coming of Christ and therefore were not asking about it. They had been told by Christ of His crucifixion and resurrection but had rebelled against any necessity for His

crucifixion (Matt. 16:21-23). Their minds were not opened to the truth of the resurrection until after it took place (Lk. 24:45-47). They expected Christ to set up an earthly kingdom but not to destroy Jerusalem and the Temple. They even sought specialplaces of honor when Christ set up His earthly kingdom, a kingdom which they mistakenly thought would free them from Rome (Mk. 10:35-37).

After the truth of the resurrection dawned upon them, their hope of an earthly kingdom was temporarily restored, and they asked Christ if He were ready to establish the kingdom of Israel (Acts 1:6). In light of the limited understanding of the disciples at the time they asked their question, (Matt. 24:3), it must be concluded that by the expression "thy coming" they were not referring to the Second Coming of the Lord. They probably had in mind His leaving Jerusalem for some place like Galilee with the expectation of His future return in judgment upon the city and Temple. They had just been shocked with what they thought was such a prediction from their Master.

Those of the fulfilled view do not, however, rule out Christ's answering the question of the disciples differently from the way it was asked. They do maintain that the main subject was the destruction of Jerusalem and that the Second Coming is not dealt with until after the time-next of Matthew 24:34 is passed.

2) The parallel passages to Matthew 24:3 do not picture a coming of the Lord; therefore, this must not be a vital part of the question. Mark records the question as if it referred to the destruction of the Temple only. He simply says, "When shall these things be? And what sign will there be when these things shall come to pass.?" (Lk.21:7). Therefore in the parallel accounts the expression "these things" had to refer to events concerning the destruction of

the Temple and not to a Second Coming or end of the age. All accounts of the one question must harmonize.

Those of the fulfilled view believe the expression in Matthew which speaks of "the end of the world" is better translated "end of the age," and refers to the end of the Jewish age or nation. This they maintain happened when Titus destroyed Jerusalem and the Temple inA.D. 70.

3) The time-text Christ gave in Matthew 24:34 demands that everything in the prophetic verses prior to it must be fulfilled within one generation after the prophecy. Jesus said, "Verily I say unto you, This generation shall not pass, till all these things be fulfilled" (Matt. 24:34). Remember the question was about "these things" (v.3), and in verse 34 Christ speaks of "these things" being fulfilled within His generation.

How long is a generation? It is the average amount of time between the birth of parents and that of their offspring. A person can use the term to apply to his span of life. The dispensational idea that generation can mean race, and the fulfillment of verse 34 can happen anytime during the existence of the Jewish race, is rejected as being without any Biblical foundation. Matthew and Christ always used the word generation to describe their contemporaries (Matt. 1:17; 11:16; 12:39-43).

When Christ was introducing His Olivet prophecy, He said, "Verily I say unto you, All these things shall come upon this generation" (Matt. 23:36). He was talking about the rejection and punishment of His contemporaries because they had gone so far as to reject His Messiahship. The Greek word *genad* is translated generation, and according to Thayer's Greek-English Lexicon of the New Testament it means "the Jewish race at one and the same period" or "the whole multitude of man at the same time." This seems to be the way Matthew always used the word (Matt. 1:17; 11:16; 12:39-43; 23:36; 24:34).

Christ was predicting something that would happen to His contemporaries. Did it happen? Yes, it happened when the Romans destroyed the city of Jerusalem and the Temple thereby ending the Jewish nation and its way of life. It all happened in A.D. 70 approximately 40 years after the prophecy was given, and according to the fulfilled view, the prophecy was then finished.

The General Signs
Matt. 24:4-13

In verse 4, Christ begins to answer the question of the disciples about when the Temple would be destroyed. Christ first gives general sign that might cause them to be misled. He wanted them to know that they could be deceived when they saw these signs being fulfilled. The potentially misleading sings included false Christs, wars, famines, pestilences, earthquakes, tribulations, family divisions, false prophets, and extensive iniquity. These signs occur in every age of history and the contemporary generation of Christ was no exception. Christ told His disciples that they could not find the answer to their question by observing these general signs.

A More specific Sign
Matt. 24:14

Christ said, "And this gospel of the kingdom shall be preached in all the world for a witness unto all nations; and then shall the end come" (Matt. 24:14). The disciples were not told that the next day after the gospel reached "all the world" that the predicted end of Jerusalem and the Temple would occur, but the implication was that the destruction would be near. In other words they could know it was close, but the sign was still vague enough that they could not tell how close.

While others may think this verse refers to the preaching of the gospel to "all the world" in an absolute sense as an end-time event, those advocating the fulfilled view do not. Neither do they think the burning of the earth by fire (2 Pet. 3:10) has any part in this prophecy. the expression "all the world" is believed to mean all the Roman world; that was all the world they knew about. That is what the expression usually means in the Bible. Luke tells us concerning the times of Christ's birth, "...That there went out a decree from Caesar Augustus, that all the world should be taxed" (Lk. 2:1). The expression "all the world" surely meant the Roman world because Caesar had no authority anywhere else.

In connection with what happened on the day of Pentecost, the Scripture states, "And there were dwelling at Jerusalem Jews, devout men, out of every nation under heaven" (Acts 2:5). Of the approximately 3,000 converts, surely many of them carried the gospel back to their nations after Pentecost was over. A little later when Christians were persecuted and scattered throughout Judea, it is said that they "...went every where preaching the word" (acts 8:4). Philip carried the gospel to Samaria (Acts 8:5) and later was instrumental in the conversion of the Ethiopian who was on his way home (Acts 8:26-40).

Paul opened his epistle to the Christians of Rome by thanking God, "... That your faith is spoken of throughout the whole world" (Rom. 1:8). By sometime in the A.D. 60s, Paul wrote his letter to the Colossians and spoke of the gospel "Which is come unto you, as it is in all the world..." (Col. 1:6) and "...which ye have heard, and which was preached to every creature which is under heaven…" (Col. 1:23). R. Bradley Jones adds:

Tradition lends its support to Paul's testimony when it says that Andrew preached the gospel in Scythia, Philip in Phrygia, Bartholomew in India, Matthew in foreign lands, James Alphaseus in Egypt, Thaddeus in Persia, Simon Zelotes in Egypt and Britain, and John Mark in Alexanderia.[1]

Thus by A.D. 70 when the Temple was destroyed, the gospel had, in Biblical terms, already reached all the world.

An Exact Sign
Matthew 24:15, 16

Jesus said to His disciples, "When ye therefore shall see the abomination of desolation, spoken of by Daniel the prophet, stand in the holy place, (whoso readeth, let him understand). Then let them which be in Judea flee into the mountains" (Matt. 24:15,16). Here Jesus gave His followers an exact sign by which they would know when it was time to flee Jerusalem. His reference to Daniel's prophecy came from Daniel 9:27 where two princes are referred to. The first prince referred to the coming Messiah (v.25) which was Christ, and the second prince was fulfilled by the Roman prince (Titus) and his army when they completely destroyed Jerusalem and the Temple.

Although Matthew did not explain who the "abomination of desolation" was, Luke lets us know that the original discussion included the party to whom Christ was referring. Luke says, "And when ye shall see Jerusalem compassed with armies, then know that the desolation thereof is nigh. Then let them which are in Judea flee to the mountains…" (Lk.21:20,21a). Remember that the disciples wanted to know when the temple would be destroyed; they wanted a sign. Jesus gave them one so unmistakably clear that not one Christian died in the destruction while over a million unbelieving Jews lost their lives from either starvation while the city gates were shut or from the storming of the city by the Roman army under Titus. Every Christian read the sign correctly, and some fled Jerusalem for mountain caves while others crossed the Jordan River to enter Pella.

The Roman army desecrated the Temple by placing ensigns there and making sacrifices to them. They then completely destroyed the city and the Temple even to the plowing up of the ground. Flavius Josephus, a non-Christian historian, gives the complete story in his work–Jewish Wars.[2] His account is long but certainly worth the time for those who want an eyewitness account of the fall of the Jewish nation.

The Great Tribulation

Matt. 24:21

Jesus said, "For then shall be great tribulation, such as was not since the beginning of the world to this time, no, nor ever shall be" (Matt. 24:21). The "great tribulation" which Christ spoke of was Jewish and applied to the time period near the destruction of Jerusalem. The expression "not since the beginning of the world to this time, no, nor ever shall be" can be taken literally or as a proverbial saying.

If taken literally, it should be applied not so much to numbers as to the intensity or nature of the suffering. The physical sufferings were so terrible that the Jews who shut themselves up in the city starved to death in great numbers. Some even turned to cannibalism with parental consumption of children. For the account of the horrible sufferings, Josephus should be consulted. He relates how people died faster than they could be buried and were simply rolled over the walls of the city.

Jewish factions within the city fought and killed one another in great numbers. Furthermore, the suffering of the Jews was more than a physical suffering. They were faced with the end of their national existence. Above all, they saw their religious way of worship totally destroyed before their eyes. Nothing is deeper than religious convictions, even when unfounded. Yes, this was the "great tribulation" of the Jews, and it was not some end-time event. Those of the fulfilled view maintain that it was not only fulfilled in A.D. 70, but it was fulfilled fully, completely, and finally.

The Elect
Matthew 24:22, 24

While speaking of the Jewish tribulation period of A.D. 70 Christ said, "and except those days should be shortened, there should no flesh be saved: but for the elect's sake those days shall be shortened" (Matt. 24:22). Who were the "elect" to whom Jesus referred? Dispensationalists tell us the term refers to Jews, but that takes the verse out of its context. It was not Jews who were saved from the destruction of Jerusalem; it was Christians who correctly read the sign Christ gave them and fled Jerusalem. Christians elsewhere in the New Testament are referred to as the elect (1 Thess. 1:4; 2 Tim. 2:10; 1 Pet. 1:2).

Christ's Coming in Judgment on Jerusalem
Matthew 24:26-34

If read alone, Matthew 24:26-34 could easily be understood as referring to the Second Coming of Christ. We are still, however, within the time-text of verse 34 which is one generation. The tribulation period referred to in verse

29 is the same tribulation spoken of in verses 16-22, a tribulation Christians escaped. Christ said, "Immediately after the tribulation of those days..." (Matt. 24:29). Whatever is described following this statement has to happen "immediately after the tribulation of those days" (v. 29) and within a generation time period (v. 34). It, therefore, could not be the end time Second Coming of Christ.

Those of the fulfilled view believe Christ simply quoted the proverbial language of the Old Testament. Isaiah predicted the downfall of Babylon with these words, "For the stars of heaven and the constellations thereof shall not give their light; the sun shall be darkened in his going forth, and the moon shall not cause her light to shine" (Isa. 13:10). This is only a proverbial description of the fall of Babylon. The sun, moon, and stars did not literally fail to shine. The light figuratively went out for the Babylonians when the Medes easily conquered them (Isa. 13:17).

Isaiah foretold the fall of Idumea with the same type of pictorial language. He said, "and all the host of heaven shall be dissolved, and the heavens shall be rolled together as a scroll: and all their host shall fall down, as the leaf falleth off from the vine, and as a falling fig from the fig tree" (Isa.34:4). This is simply poetic language used to describe the fall of a nation.

Another prophet, Ezekiel, foretold the fall of Egypt in similar poetic language. He said "...I will cover the heaven, and make the stars thereof dark; I will cover the sun with a cloud, and the moon shall not give her light. All the bright lights of heaven will I make dark over thee..." (Ezek. 32:7,8). With those pictorial words the prophet described the light being extinguished in a great nation, that is, her fall.

Those of the fulfilled view often present other examples, but the idea is that Christ simply used the language He inspired the prophets to use earlier. He used the same language to foretell the destruction of national Israel in A.D. 70 that Old Testament prophets had used to foretell the destruction of Egypt, Babylon, Idumea, etc.

Matthew 24:36-51

A few interpret the rest of Matthew 24 as referring to the destruction of Jerusalem also, but the majority, including postmillennialists, think that Christ now had His Second Coming in mind. There is no real problem with this switch once the time-text, verse 34, is passed. Even though the disciples did not have His Second Coming in mind when they referred to "thy coming" (v. 3), Christ perhaps wanted to give them some information which if not understood immediately would be meaningful to them later. They would not understand the Second Coming concept until they were forced to give up the idea of an earthly kingdom.

Due to dispensational teachings, it is necessary to comment on two verses from this passage. Jesus said, "Then two shall be in the field; the one shall be taken, and the other one left. Two women shall be grinding at the mill; the one shall be taken, and the other left" (Matt. 24:40, 41). Dispensationalists constantly maintain that Christ here taught that when the pretribulation rapture comes, the righteous will be taken up into Heaven while the lost will be left to experience the great tribulation period. The truth is that these verses do not say that.

First of all, Christ did not say whether the lost or saved would be taken first. He only said that one would be taken first and the other left. If the primary reference here is to the Second Coming, His primary thought was probably that of separation, not necessarily who would be dealt with first. If by chance He did have order in mind, He may very well have thought in terms of the wicked being taken first rather than the righteous. He had taught this in several places (Matt. 13:30, 39, 41-43, 49,50).

If the reference is primarily to the destruction of Jerusalem rather than His Second Coming, Christ could have meant that the calamity would be sudden, and those not watching would be captured before they realized that they were in danger.

Futurist View

The futurists believe that "thy coming" in verse 3 refers to the yet future personal and visible return of Christ after the end-time tribulation period. This is not applied to any rapture of the church phase of His Second Coming. Christ's Second Coming is generally given as the only possible meaning; no other possibility is mentioned. Verse 14 is always given as a proof text for world-wide evangelization just prior to the Second Coming. The fulfilled view is totally ignored. The "abomination of desolation" (v. 15) is pictured as an end-time antichrist, not as a Roman army which destroyed Jerusalem in A.D. 70. The great tribulation period (v. 21) is said to be yet future and will take place just prior to Christ's Second Coming. The futurists do not talk about any Jewish tribulation period connected with the destruction because the elect (v. 22) are said to be the Jews, not Christians. Jews are therefore supposed to be saved, not destroyed.

Matthew 24:23-31 is frequently presented as proof of the yet future Second Coming of the Lord with not a hint of any other possible interpretation. The fulfilled view time-text (v. 34) is quickly explained by making "generation" equal race, nation, or Israel. Therefore they say that the Jewish race will not pass away before the predictions of verses 1-33 are fulfilled. There is no proof that the word translated "generation" is used in the Bible to mean race or nation, but this does not stop the continuous claim. On the other hand, those who hold the fulfilled view give several passages showing that Matthew used the word to refer to the people living at the time of Christ.

In spite of these somewhat opposite ways of interpreting Matthew 24:1-34, there is no serious difference over interpreting the rest of the chapter except concerning the dispensational claims in respect to verses 40 and 41. This has already been explained and will not be repeated here. All premillennialists hold to a futurist view but not an identical one.

Past, Present, Future View

Amillennialists usually follow this past, present, and future view. Some amillennialists, however, agree with postmillennialists on this issue and see everything in Matthew 24:1-34 as history. The majority maintains that the Olivet prophecy was fulfilled, but not completely so.

William Cox, an amillennialists, explains it thusly:

Many prophecies have a dual meaning, which is to say that there is a primary fulfillment in the historical setting in which the prophecy is made, then a secondary fulfillment which usually has more of a spiritual (though deeper) fulfillment. Perhaps the prophecy of Matthew 24 comes under this category.[3]

Concerning the Olivet Discourse, Hoekema comments:

Jesus gives a number of signs which had their initial fulfillment at the time of the destruction of Jerusalem; since this discourse exemplifies the principle of prophetic foreshortening, however, the signs mentioned in them will have a further fulfillment at the time of the Parousia.[4]

One thing that makes the Olivet Discourse difficult to interpret is that Jesus refers definitely to the destruction of

Jerusalem in some parts but seems to point to His Second Coming in other parts. In fact, the aspects of these two different events are so intermingled that it is difficult to determine which one He is talking about or whether He might be talking about both by way of double reference.

According to this past, present, and future view of Matthew 24, the words "thy coming" (v. 3) can refer to either or both His coming in judgment upon the Jewish nation in A.D. 70 and His climatic Second Coming. It is generally admitted, however, that the disciples did not comprehend the Second Coming very well. The signs (vv. 4-13) are general and happen in all periods of history.

The prediction that "all the world" (v. 14) would hear the gospel before the "end" is interpreted as being fulfilled prior to and at the destruction of Jerusalem. That does not, however, rule out another fulfillment at the end-time. The same is true of the abomination of desolation" (v. 15), the great tribulation (v. 21) and the coming of Christ (vv.23-31). Some feel that certain events, such as the great tribulation, must be stretched out across history because it affected the people in A.D. 70, yet it was said that Christ would come "immediately" after the tribulation (v. 29). The fulfilled view solves this by saying verses 29-31 do not refer to the Second Coming of Christ, but those of the past, present, and future view do not agree. While they may admit that these verses do not apply to the Second Coming of Christ exclusively; nevertheless, they see it in the verses.

The time-text (v.34) does not have the same significance to those of the past, present, and future view as it does to those of the fulfilled view. While admitting that "all these things" were fulfilled in that generation, a future fulfillment is not ruled out. The views on the rest of the chapter have already been sufficiently explained.

What shall we say to conclude Matthew 24? If the reader is still confused, he might find some comfort in the fact that the Disciples of Christ after listening to the discourse probably felt the same way. This author feels that one should be very careful in trying to establish doctrine from this difficult discourse. Even when a second fulfillment is possible, without divine revelation, caution is called for. Because a thing is possible does not mean it is necessary. In other words, if one wants to believe in an end-time, world-wide evangelism, a future antichrist, a future tribulation period, etc., his proof-text should not come from Matthew 24. Matthew 24 should be used as secondary support rather than as the primary proof-text.

Revelation 3:10

In a specific message to the church in Philadelphia, Christ said:

Behold, I will make them of the synagogue of Satan, which say they are Jews, and are not, but do lie; behold, I will make them to come and worship before thy feet, and to know that I have loved thee. Because thou hast kept the word of my patience, I also will keep thee from the hour of temptation, which shall come upon all the world, to try them that dwell upon the earth (Rev. 3:9,10).

Clarence Larkin, a dispensational premillennialist, claims the ability to teach "dispensational truth" and to "rightly divide" the Word. When commenting concerning the church in Philadelphia and Revelation 3:10, he wrote:

It was to be kept from the "Hour of Temptation" (TRIBULATION), that shall come upon ALL THE WORLD, and as there has never yet been a WORLDWIDE Tribulation, this "Hour of Temptation" must still be future and refers to the "Great Tribulation" that is to come upon the "whole world" just before the return of the Lord to set up His Millennial Kingdom, and as the promise is that the "Philadelphia Church" shall not pass through the Tribulation, is not this additional proof that the Church shall be "caught out" before the Tribulation?

The Philadelphia Period covers the time between A.D. 1750 and A.D. 1900. We must not forget that the characteristics of all Periods continue on in the church down to the end.[5]

While Dr. Larkin claims to rightly divide the Word, Revelation 3:10 is subject to an interpretation somewhat different from his so-called dispensational truth. First, it seems clear that Christ addressed the church in Philadelphia that existed at the time the Book of Revelation was written, and not a worldwide church that was to be raptured out of tribulation prior to an earthly millennium. While Larkin mentions "WORLDWIDE" tribulation that is yet future, the "Great Tribulation" just prior to the Lord's return, the setting up of the "MILLENNIAL KINGDOM," and the church being "caught out: before the tribulation, the verse in question does not mention any of these. Is this rightly dividing the Word?

Christ addressed a local church (Philadelphia) that was faced with Judaizers who falsely claimed to be true Israelites. In opposition to these Jewish claims, Christ presented Himself as the "holy" and "true" Messiah (v. 7) that was the fulfilled promise of the Old Testament Jewish prophets. These Judaizers claimed to be the real Jews of promise, but Jesus said they were of the "synagogue of Satan" (v. 9) and that their claim based upon fleshly Israel rather than spiritual Israel was a lie. The massage is that they would have to submit to Christians rather than being able to force Christians to submit to them.

Christ did speak of an "hour of temptation" that would come upon all the world (v. 10), but that does not necessarily mean WORLDWIDE as we presently use the word. We have already discussed what the expression, "all the world" meant at the time the Bible was written, and it is not necessary to restate it here. Christ also said that He would "keep them from the hour of temptation," but that can certainly happen without a rapture. It may simply mean that the Philadelphia church would be kept from sinking under a test that some would fail (v. 9). Furthermore, there is absolutely no indication that by the "temptation" (v. 10) Christ meant an end-time great tribulation period prior to a millennium and before which Christians would be raptured out of the world.

Revelation 7:14

An elder in a vision said to John, "...these are they which came out of great tribulation, and have washed their robes, and made them white in the blood of the Lamb" (Rev. 7:14). The people referred to were up in Heaven and were introduced as, "...A great multitude, which no man could number, of all nations, and kindreds, and people, and tongues, stood before the throne, and before the Lamb..." (Rev. 7:9). Under the protection of the Lamb, they are now very happy and secure.

The primary question for consideration is, what is meant by the expression, "come out of great tribulation" (v.14)? First, it needs to be pointed out that the verb tense indicates continuous action, not completed action. The idea is that they had been coming out of great tribulation and were continuing to do so. Several modern translations reflect this idea. Nevertheless, the question is, to what tribulation is the writer referring? There are several views.

1. The dispensational view is that it refers to Daniel's 70th week of prophecy, a seven-year period between what they call the "rapture" and the "revelation" of Christ. Dispensationalists say it does not concern the church because it will be gone to Heaven before the great tribulation and the antichrist appear. On assumptions, and without any

Scriptural foundation, this view is generally presented as if it were the only possible interpretation. Some speak of the great tribulation as only the last half of the assumed seven-year period. When explaining this tribulation period (vv. 9,14) Clarence Larkin, a dispensationalist, stated:

This "Blood Washed Multitude" introduces us to another class of the saved of the "End-Time". They do not represent the Church, for the Church has already been taken out. ...The statement that they "came out of great tribulation" does not necessarily imply that it was "The Great Tribulation," that they came out of, for that covers only the "last half" of the Week, and they are seen by John in the middle of the "first half" of the Week.[6]

Of course, Dr. Larkin is assuming Daniel's 70th week of prophecy is future, that there will be a rapture before the tribulation period, and that everything in Revelation 4-19 is confined to a future seven-year tribulation, etc. According to this dispensational view, during the first half of a future seven-year tribulation period, without either the convicting power of the Holy Spirit or the church, a multitude so large that no man can number (v.9) will be saved. With modern calculators man can count huge numbers of people. It is strange that what the church under the anointing of the Holy Spirit could not do in ages, will somehow be accomplished in a future three and one half year period. Accordingly, the gospel of the kingdom minus the cross is much more powerful than the gospel of grace with its cross. Reader, beware!

2. A second view of the "Great Tribulation" of Revelation 7:14 is that it refers to the "great tribulation" of A.D. 70 (Matt. 24:21).

3. A third view is that the "Great Tribulation" of Revelation 7:14 refers to a tribulation period lasting approximately 250 years beginning with Nero in A.D. 64 and ending with the edict of Constantine in A.D. 313.

4. A fourth view is that the "Great Tribulation" of Revelation 7:14 refers to persecutions of every kind and is continuous. Christians have suffered tribulation since the beginning of Christianity and will continue to do so (Jn. 16:33). Paul taught that "...we must though much tribulation enter into the kingdom of God" (Acts 14:22). This view, therefore, makes the "Great Tribulation" the sum of all tribulations of every type.

In light of these various views, it is therefore questionable to establish the idea of an exclusive end-time tribulation from Revelation 7:14.

Chapter Summary

We have surveyed the six most frequently used passages to establish the doctrine of an exclusive end-time tribulation period and found the evidence much less than often thought. Evidence may not be totally lacking, but it is vague. An end-time tribulation period can be established by using the concept of double referencing. However, this could be dangerous. A prophecy *may* have more than one fulfillment, but that does not mean that it *must* have more than one fulfillment.

Perhaps the strongest evidence favoring an end-time tribulation period is not found in the preceding six Scriptural passages, but in the account of the loosing of Satan for a "little season" (Rev. 20:3,7). This passage was examined in the previous chapter concerning the "man of sin" or antichrist, and the reader is referred back to that discussion. It should be understood that when people establish an end-time antichrist and tribulation on the basis of Revelation 20:3,7, they are not talking about the dispensational end-time tribulations, etc. This climatic tribulation had nothing to do with Daniel's 70th week of prophecy, a rapture of the church, or an event of any type that precedes a millennium.

Finally, it should be remembered that neither premillennialism, postmillennialism, nor amillennialism stands or falls because of one's view concerning an antichrist or a particular type of tribulation period. Premillennialists have pretribulationists, midtribulationists, and posttribulationists in their camp. They also have some who teach a partial rapture theory. Amillennialists generally believe in an end-time antichrist and tribulation period but not identical to those of premillennialists. Some amillennialists believe in the fulfilled view similar to postmillennialists. The postmillennialists are the most consistent of the three, but even their camp is not absolute.

Each of the three major millennial systems of thought can, therefore, allow variety concerning antichrists and tribulation without being destroyed as a distinct system.

Chapter 8

Prophecy and the Resurrection

Eschatology and the bodily resurrection are essentially united. There is more said in the Bible about the resurrection of the righteous than of the unrighteous; nevertheless, the resurrection of both is taught. The big question concerns whether or not there will be one final bodily resurrection which includes both the righteous and the unrighteous, or if there will be a series of resurrections separated by time.

There are actually two resurrections (not bodily resurrections) taught in the Scriptures. One is a spiritual resurrection which begins with the new birth and includes the going to be with the Lord in soul form at death. This spiritual resurrection is referred to in several passages (Eph. 2:1, 4-6; Col. 2:13, 3:1; 1 Tim. 5:6; 1 Jn. 4:14; Jn. 5:24, 25; Rev. 20:4,5), but it is outside our purpose to deal extensively with the spiritual resurrection except in the questionable passage of Revelation 20.

Most of the time when people think of the resurrection, they are only thinking of the bodily resurrection. This may be the reason the writer of Revelation 20:5 specifically used the term "first resurrection"; he wanted to make sure people were thinking in terms other than the normal bodily resurrection. This would perhaps be the best way to do so since the word "resurrection" is always singular in the Bible. Since people think in terms of a bodily resurrection that is singular, what better way is there to draw their attention to the spiritual or soul resurrection than by using the term "first resurrection" to refer to it?

Postmillennialists and amillennialists agree that the Bible only pictures one general bodily resurrection; that is, both the righteous and the unrighteous (believers and unbelievers) will be resurrected at the same time. This will take place at the parousia or Second Coming of Christ at the last day.

The historic posttribulation premillennialists believe in at least two separate bodily resurrections, one prior to a 1,000 year earthly reign of Christ and the other after it. The dispensational pretribulation premillennialists, however, must increase the number of bodily resurrections. They frequently teach that there will be four separate bodily resurrections – 1) one for the church at the rapture prior to a tribulation period, 2) one after the tribulation period but prior to the millennium so the dead tribulation saints can have a part in the millennium, 3) one after the millennium for those converted during that time, and 4) one for the wicked dead following the millennium and at the end of time as we know it.

Therefore, dispensationalists have a single resurrection stretched into four different resurrections: three for the righteous and one for the unrighteous. When these read about the resurrection in the Bible, they have to decide which of the four resurrections is under discussion, and this complicates interpretations.

It is not claimed, however, that all dispensationalists believe in four different resurrections. Some eliminate the second resurrection following the tribulation period by maintaining that the millennium will not have any resurrected people in it; it will be confined to living people on earth who happen to be both alive and saved at the end of the tribulation and at the revelation of Christ. The millennium is therefore only for saints living through the tribulation period. This view, however, leaves some dead tribulation saints for a future resurrection. Still others eliminate the third resurrection for those saved during the millennium. They do this by including them in the resurrection when the wicked are resurrected (Rev. 20:11-15). There seems to be a very small number of dispensationalists who fit into this last category. Dispensationalists generally insist that Revelation 20:11-15 applies only to the wicked.

Which of the preceding concepts is taught in the Bible? Will there be a single resurrection which includes both the just and the unjust, a two-stage resurrection separated by 1,000 years, or a four-stage resurrection –three for the righteous and one for the wicked? It is herein maintained that the Bible teaches a single resurrection that will include all people –saved or lost, Jew or Gentile, etc.

Righteous and Unrighteous Together

Anyone who wishes to arrive at the truth concerning whether or not there will be a general resurrection, must go first to the Scriptures that deal with the resurrection of both the righteous and the unrighteous. Once this is done, they must then look to see if both groups are raised at the same hour or if there is a time gap between their resurrections.

Paul and other Biblical writers frequently wrote to churches that they had previously established and answered inquiries from them. At times, therefore, it was not the purpose of writers to deal with both believers and unbelievers. They sometimes deal only with problems of believers and speak only in terms of the believer's resurrection. This does not mean that the unbeliever will not be resurrected at the same time; it simply means it was not the purpose of the writer to talk about the unrighteous. One could follow the same reasoning and conclude that Christ did not wash His disciples' feet during the Passion Week because neither Matthew, Mark nor Luke mentioned it. John, however, did mention it, and it did take place.

Daniel 12:2

Although the doctrine of a resurrection is not frequently spoken of in the Old Testament, Daniel does refer to it and includes in it both the righteous and the unrighteous. He says, "And many of them that sleep in the dust of the earth shall awake, some to everlasting life, and some to shame and everlasting contempt" (Dan. 12:2). Daniel, therefore, explicitly speaks of a bodily resurrection (singular) of the dead. There were, however, two classes of people in this single resurrection. One class, the righteous, awake to everlasting life (Heaven); while the other class, the unrighteous, awake to everlasting contempt (Hell or punishment). Daniel placed no time period between the resurrection of the righteous and the unrighteous because no such time period existed. To claim there must be at least 1,000 years between these events is to destroy the language of the writer.

The premillennial system demands that a long time period be inserted between the resurrection of the righteous and the unrighteous. To avoid the insertion of at least 1,000 years, some deny that Daniel was even talking about a bodily resurrection. They believe what Daniel had in mind was that Jews who were scattered over the world would return to Israel; that is, they were going to be in a sense resurrected from foreign lands. These are the same interpreters who advise others not to spiritualize the Scriptures but take them for just what they say.

John 5:28, 29

We come now to the words of Jesus and the clearest passage in the Bible on the subject of the bodily resurrection of the dead. The words of Christ are in clear harmony with those of Daniel. Christ said:

Marvel not at this: for the hour is coming, in the which all that are in the graves shall hear his voice, And shall come forth; they that have done good, unto the resurrection of life; and they that have done evil, unto the resurrection of damnation (Jn. 5:28,29).

Notice that an "hour" is coming when "all that are in the graves" (dead) shall hear the voice of Christ as He calls them in one general resurrection from the graves. Christ clearly says all the dead will hear His voice in a specific "hour", but premillennialists say they all do not hear His voice at one time. As has already been explained, dispensationalists often say some of the righteous (the church) will hear Christ's call from the grave at a rapture prior to the seven-year tribulation period; another righteous group will hear His voice 1,000 years later at the end of a millennium; and finally the wicked will hear His voice just prior to the Great White Throne Judgment and just before being cast into the lake of fire forever (Rev. 20:11-15).

Why did not Christ say there were several resurrections if that is what He meant? He teaches in the clearest of language that all will come out of the tombs at the same time, but then they will be judged so that they head in two different directions. After judgment the righteous will receive Heaven and the unrighteous Hell. There is absolutely no hint of 1,000 years or 1,007 years between resurrections; it is a single resurrection with two classes of people in it, believers and unbelievers.

Dispensationalists remind us that the word "hour" does not have to be taken literally and point to the "hour" in

John 5:25; an hour they claim is parallel to John 5:28. The spiritual resurrection is under discussion in verse 25, not a bodily resurrection. It is true that the "hour" of verse 25 keeps repeating itself down through history every time a person is regenerated or born again; with each new birth there is a new spiritual resurrection. The fact is, however, these two resurrections or hours are not truly parallel.

If they were parallel, there would have to be a bodily resurrection every day since there is a spiritual resurrection somewhere daily. According to premillennialists there will be two, three, or four bodily resurrections but not daily resurrections. There will not be several hours or calls; the voice of Christ will call one time, and all the dead will hear it, both the good and the evil (v.29). The verse is not emphasizing two different times for people to be raised; it emphasizes two different kinds of people to be raised.

In summary, all the dead hear the voice of Christ at the same hour, come forth from the grave at the same hour, and are separated during the same hour. Only in people's imagination is there 1,000 or 1,007 years between the resurrection of the righteous and the unrighteous. In Daniel 12:2 and in John 5:28,29 the righteous and the unrighteous are resurrected at the same time. There is yet another New Testament passage that teaches the same truth.

Acts 24:15

Paul while defending himself said, "And have hope toward God, which they themselves also allow, that there shall be a resurrection of the dead, both of the just and the unjust" (Acts 24:15). The Jews were divided on the issue of a resurrection; the Pharisees believed there would be one while the Sadducees denied it. Paul was at least attempting to get the Pharisees on his side.

Paul's statement seems simple enough. He said there would be a resurrection (singular) of the dead (not part of the dead). This single resurrection would consist of two kinds of people, the "just and the unjust." This harmonizes perfectly with what Daniel and Christ had already taught. To turn a single resurrection into two, three, or four resurrections is incredible. To illustrate, what if one changed the words "just and unjust" to males and females or blacks and whites? Would this mean it should be assumed that males and females or blacks and whites would have resurrections at least 1,000 year apart?

If Daniel 12:2; John 5:28,29; and Acts 24:15 do not describe a general bodily resurrection for all dead people (good or evil) at the same hour, then language cannot be found to do so.

There are a number of other Scriptures which imply that the righteous and unrighteous remain together until the end (Matt. 13:30,39,49,50; 16:27; 25:31,32; 2 Thess. 1:7-10; Rev. 20:12,13). The resurrection of the just and the unjust cannot be separated by a thousand years or more because they both remain together until the end of the world (Matt. 13:30, 39-43).

Job 14:10-12

The earliest Biblical account of the time of the bodily resurrection is found in the Book of Job. It says:

But man dieth, and wasteth away: yea, man giveth up the ghost, and where is he? As the waters fail from the sea, and the flood decayeth and drieth up: So man lieth down, and riseth not: till the heavens be no more, they shall not awake, nor be raised out of their sleep (Job 14:10-12).

How long is the body going to remain in the grave? Notice that Job under inspiration answered "till the heavens be no more." Mankind will awake, but not before the heavens pass away. When will this be? It is always pictured as the last event before the eternal state. Peter says:

> But the day of the Lord will come as a thief in the night; in which the heavens shall pass away with a great noise, and the elements shall melt with fervent heat, the earth also and the works that are therein shall be burned up. Seeing then that all these things shall be dissolved, what manner of persons ought ye to be in all holy conversation and godliness, Looking for and hasting unto the coming of the day of God, wherein the heavens being on fire shall be dissolved, and the elements shall melt with fervent heat? Nevertheless we, according to his promise, look for new heavens and a new earth, wherein dwelleth righteousness (2 Pet. 3:10-13).

It cannot be denied that the passing away of the present heavens and earth and the creation of new ones is an end-time event connected to the Second Coming of the Lord. Revelation 20:11 and 21:1 also make it clear that this is true. Job, Peter, and John while under inspiration each spoke of the same end-time event.

Peter told his readers to look for the coming of Christ at which time the old heavens and earth would pass away and new ones would be created (2 Pet. 3:14). How could they look for this event, when according to dispensationalists, they are supposed to be raptured 1,007 years prior, and according to historical premillennialists 1,000 years before this event? Remember the eternal state, not a millennium, follows the creation of a new Heaven and earth (Rev. 21:1).

Prior to Peter's prediction of the Lord's coming and His burning the earth he had said, "Knowing this first, that there will come in the last days scoffers, walking after their own lusts, And saying, Where is the promise of his coming? For since the father fell asleep, all things continue as they were from the beginning" (2 Pet. 3:3,4). How is it that the scoffers will be on earth during or after the tribulation and millennium, and yet had never heard of Christ's coming? Will Christ rapture all the saints from the earth resulting in the unbelievable airplane crashes, automobiles wrecks, bus wrecks, truck wrecks, train wrecks, etc. without people at the end-time having any knowledge of why these wrecks happen or why all Christian operators, etc. vanished from the earth? It would seem that the rapture, the great tribulation, and Christ's rule of iron would have gotten their attention. Yet the scoffers are predicted to claim there is no sign of the coming of Christ prior to this burning of the earth.

The truth is that Peter did not know anything about a rapture of the church or an earthly millennium when he wrote 2 Peter 3 and challenged his readers to look for the coming of the Lord, the passing of the present heavens and earth, and the creation of a new eternal state. He did, under inspiration, write about what Job had earlier been inspired to reveal.

After Job prophesied that man would not rise from the grave "till the heavens be no more," he went on to say, "Thou shalt call, and I will answer thee" (Job 14:15). Job expected to rise after the heavens passed, not at a pretribulation rapture or at a revelation of Christ prior to an earthly millennium.

Job explained further in a later passage by saying, "For I know that my redeemer liveth, and that he shall stand at the latter day upon the earth: And though after my skin worms destroy this body, yet in my flesh shall I see God" (Job 19:25,26). Job said he would not rise from dead and see the Lord until the Lord stood upon the earth. This, of course, would rule out his having any part in a pretribulation rapture when Christ is said to come only in the air and not to earth. In fairness to dispensationalists, it should be pointed out that at least some of them teach that all Old Testament saints miss the rapture, an event they say is for the Christian church only.

This does not solve the conflict, however, for dispensationalists often have the Old Testament and tribulation saints rising from the dead prior to an earthly millennium. Job, on the other hand, said that he did not expect to rise "till the heavens be no more."

The Righteous at Christ's Coming

It was pointed out earlier that more is said in the Bible about the resurrection of the righteous than of the wicked. However, where they are mentioned together they are not separated in time. New Testament writers frequently wrote to answer questions from their Christian contemporaries. These questions often did not concern the future of the wicked; therefore, they were left out of the discussion.

Luke 14:14

Luke does speak of the resurrection of the just in his Gospel without at the same time referring to the resurrection of the unjust. He says, "…For thou shalt be recomposed at the resurrection of the just" (Lk. 14:14). Luke is actually quoting Christ, and Christ was challenging the righteous to be good to the poor, blind, lame, etc. Christ was not dealing with the wicked and therefore did not mention their resurrection. That does not at all prove that it will not take place at the same time as the resurrection of the righteous. Luke does mention the resurrection of the just and the unjust together when quoting Paul, and at that time he did not separate them in time (Acts 24:15).

Furthermore, it can be determined from other Scriptures when the resurrection of the just will take place.

It will happen at the Second Coming of Christ at the last day (Jn. 6:39,40,44,54). Notice that the Bible in all these verses places the resurrection of the just "at the last day," not during the last days. These verses read as follows:

And this is the Father's will which hath sent me, that of all which he hath given me I should lose nothing, but should raise it up again AT THE LAST DAY (Jn. 6:39).

And this is the will of him that seen me, that every one which seeth the Son, and believeth on him, may have everlasting life: and I will raise him up AT THE LAST DAY (Jn 6:40).

No man can come to me, except the Father which hath sent me draw him; and I will raise him up AT THE LAST DAY (Jn. 6:44).

Whoso eateth my flesh, and drinketh my blood, hath eternal life; and I will raise him up AT THE LAST DAY (Jn. 6:54).

The premillennial system of thought will not harmonize with the preceding verses. Premillennialists teach that the wicked will be resurrected at the last day, but the righteous will be resurrected either 1,007 or 1,000 years before the last day. Of course, premillennialists try in some way to spiritualize the "last day" and make it cover hundreds of years, but that is forcing the language to justify their system of thought.

Not only are the righteous going to be resurrected at the last day, but Jesus says that is exactly when the wicked are going to be judged. Christ said, "…the word that I have spoken, the same shall judge him in the last day" (Jn. 12:48). Why are the wicked dealt with at the last day just like the righteous? Because there is no day after the last day.

While Luke 14:14 does speak of the resurrection of the just, it offers absolutely no proof that there will be a resurrection of the wicked at least 1,000 years later.

I Thessalonians 4:13-17

The church at Thessalonica has a problem concerning the coming of the Lord. Since Christ had not come quickly, they were not sure what this meant for their fellow Christians who had died. Would living Christians have any advantage over the dead Christians? Was there actually any hope for the Christians who had died? Paul answered their inquiry by saying:

But I would not have you to be ignorant, brethren, concerning them which are asleep, that ye sorrow not, even as others which have no hope. For if we believe that Jesus died and rose again, even so they also which sleep in Jesus will God bring with him. For this we say unto you by the word of the Lord, that we which are alive and remain unto the coming of the lord shall not prevent then which are asleep. For the Lord himself shall descend from heaven with a shout, with the voice of the archangel, and with the trump of God: and the dead in Christ shall rise first: Then we which are alive and remain shall be caught up together with them in the clouds to meet the Lord in the air: and so shall we ever be with the Lord (1 Thess. 4:13-17).

Dispensationalists let their imaginations run wild when they read this passage. They produce films of Christ's Second Coming with tremendous airplane crashes, automobile wrecks, truck wrecks, bus wrecks, train wrecks, etc., all because Christian drivers, pilots, and conductors are secretly raptured away. It is sometimes pictured as a quiet and secret coming that leaves the lost wondering what happened to their companions, etc.

Not only are we told that this is a secret coming, but we are told that it is the coming of Christ in the air "for" His saints, not "with" them. He will come "with" them at His revelation seven years later.

Frequently great emphasis is placed upon the expression, "and the dead in Christ shall rise first" (v.16).

They maintain that this is proof from the Word of God that the righteous will rise 1,007 years (a tribulation period plus a millennium) before the wicked will be resurrected.

How shall we answer these argument? First, all the big crashes are nothing but fantasy. There is not one hint in this passage to support the big wrecks. Furthermore, this coming of the Lord is not pictured as something secret and quiet. The Lord descends with a noisy shout which is loud enough to wake up all the dead (Jn. 5:28,29); then will be the voice of the archangel and the sounding of the great trump of God (v.16).

The argument that this is a pretribulation coming "for" and not "with" His saints is absolutely contradictory to the passage itself. It says, "...Even so them also which sleep in Jesus will God bring WITH him" (v.14). When introducing the materials of this chapter, Paul in the last verse of the preceding chapter said, "To the end he may stablish your hearts unblamable in holiness before God, even our Father, at the coming of our Lord Jesus Christ WITH all his saints" (1 Thess. 3:13).

The expression, "and the dead in Christ shall rise first" (v.16), in taken totally out of context. Paul is not comparing the dead in Christ to the wicked outside of Christ. The word "first" (v.16) is correlative to the following word "then" (v.17) which introduces the second group the writer has in mind. That second group was not the wicked dead, but it was instead the righteous living. In its context the whole passage is contrasting what will happen to two groups when Christ comes. These two groups are dead believers and living believers, and Paul assures the Thessalonian church that the living will have no advantage over dead believers. They will rise to meet the Lord together, and Paul says, "...and so shall we ever be with the Lord" (v.17).

When speaking concerning the expression, "and the dead in Christ shall rise first," Everett Carver said, "Efforts to make this text say that the wicked will be resurrected later is either the result of ignorance or is prompted by a desire to deceive. Neither should be connected with biblical exegesis."[1]

The expression, "and so shall we ever be with the Lord" (v.17), creates another problem for many dispensationalists. The expression seems to clearly teach that wherever Christ is there also will be His resurrected believers. However, many dispensationalists deny that any resurrected people will take part in Christ's 1,000 year reign from Jerusalem. They are left somewhere in Heaven (perhaps the New Jerusalem) while Jesus is on earth. The claim itself (that there will be no resurrected people in the millennium) is somewhat contradictory since Jesus is a resurrected being.

While 1 Thessalonians 4:13-17 does speak of the resurrection of the righteous without any reference to the resurrection of the wicked, there is no proof whatsoever that they are resurrected 1,000 or 1,007 years apart. It simply was not the purpose of the writer to deal with the resurrection of the unrighteous.

In Paul's next letter to this church he does, however, imply that when the Lord comes He will deal with the unbelievers and believers at the same time. He wrote:

And to you who are troubled rest with us, when the Lord Jesus shall be revealed from heaven with his mighty angels, In flaming fire taking vengeance on them that know not God, and that obey not the gospel of our Lord Jesus Christ: Who shall be punished with everlasting destruction from the presence of the Lord, and from the glory of his power; WHEN he shall come to be glorified in his saints... (2Thess. 1:7-10).

Paul, in Acts, made clear his belief in one general resurrection with both the just and the unjust present (Acts 24:15).

Philippians 3:11

Paul said, "If by any means I might attain unto the resurrection of the dead" (Phil.3:11). It may be difficult to know all and exactly what Paul had in mind when he spoke these words. He surely is not expressing doubt about the resurrection; he has made that plain in his other writings. *Exanastasis,* the Greek word Paul used here for resurrection, is not found elsewhere in the New Testament. It would appear from the surrounding verses that Paul was desiring a perfect state that he had not yet attained. He was striving for it like a hard working athlete would strive to be a winner, but he did not yet have the ultimate prize. He was saved but desired more than salvation. Christ had been resurrected to the ultimate state, and this is what Paul longed for (vs. 20,21). Not even the intermediate state during which the soul is with the Lord is the ultimate state. Man is not complete without a body to house the spirit. Paul yearned for that time; it would be far superior to anything obtainable during this life.

Paul does seem to be referring to the resurrection of the righteous but there is no hint that it is separated from the resurrection of the unrighteous. Some try to change the King James translation by adding the word "among" and making the passage read, "Resurrected from among the dead." Then they imply that the part of the dead are left behind. Some claim that Paul was striving to attain unto the resurrection of the righteous in order to share in the millennium. This is putting words in Paul's mouth. While there may be some doubt as to exactly what Paul meant, that does not mean that this verse supports premillennialism in any form. It is not claimed that all premillennialists use this verse as a proof text that Paul was desiring to be in a millennium, because some dispensationalists do not believe any resurrected persons will share in the millennium.

1 Corinthians 15:23,24

In the midst of this chapter on the subject of the resurrection Paul says, "But every man in his own order: Christ the first fruits; afterwards they that are Christ's at his coming. Then cometh the end..." (1 Cor. 15:23,24). We are told by some that Paul here attempts to explain the order of the resurrection which had three stages. First, Christ is resurrected; second (after much time expires" Christ comes and resurrects all that are Christians; and finally after a millennium the resurrection of the wicked transpires. It is claimed that the Greek word *eita* translated "then" (v.24) does not mean immediately; it simply means later on and in this case 1,000 or 1,007 years later on.

It is herein maintained that this is not the correct interpretation. Paul gives two orders to the resurrection, not three. Christ, the Captain, is resurrected first. Second, those who belong to Christ are resurrected at His Second Coming. The unrighteous do not belong to Christ and are not under discussion. This does not mean the wicked will not be resurrected at Christ's Second Coming; it only means that Paul's purpose at that time was to deal with the righteous or those who belong to Christ.

The expression, "Then cometh the end..." (v. 24) does not introduce a third order of the resurrection. It does not say or mean the end of the resurrection. It simply means that when Christ comes and resurrects the righteous, this world as we know it will end. This interpretation harmonizes with Scriptures in general. Christ ends, rather than begins, His kingdom when He comes again (v.24).

Christ will be ready for those who are His to inherit a spiritual body prepared for the eternal state.

What about the argument that *eita* (v.24) translated "then" does not mean immediately but later on, and in this case at least 1,000 years later on? The Greek word *eita* is translated "then" ten times in the New Testament, but in no place does it refer to a long period such as a millennium (Lk. 8:12; Jn.19:27; 20:27; 1 Cor. 12:28; 15:5,7,24; 1 Tim. 2:13; 3:10; James 1:15). When Paul intended a long time period such as the time period between the resurrection of Christ and the resurrection of those who belong to Christ, he used another word *epeita* rather than *eita*for the word "then" (v.23). While the word *eita* may not always mean immediately, it does mean that which is next and follows almost immediately. Forcing this word to cover a period of a thousand years is unnatural and not justifiable.

The truth is, that, if Paul wanted to say anything about a millennium, he passed up a wonderful opportunity, especially when he was trying to reveal an important time order. If he had desired to say anything about the millennium, he would have done so, but he did not either here or elsewhere. This passage offers no proof that the resurrection of the righteous and the unrighteous is separated by a millennium. When the resurrection of the righteous occurs, then the end comes. 1 Corinthians 15:23,24 is a chief proof passages of premillennialists, and yet it offers little support for their eschatology.

1 Corinthians 15:50-52

Paul continues in this chapter with his teaching concerning the resurrection of believers. He wrote:

Now this I say, brethren, that flesh and blood cannot inherit the kingdom of God; neither doth corruption inherit incorruption. Behold, I shew you a mystery; We shall not all sleep, but we shall

Dr. Cecil Sanders
Eschatology: End-Time Views Compared

all be changed, In a moment, in the twinkling of an eye, at the last trump: for the trumpet shall sound, and the dead shall be raised incorruptible, and we shall be changed (1 Cor. 15:50-52).

Paul is discussing the kingdom of God in its eternal aspect, the kingdom of God after Christ delivers up His kingdom to the Father (v. 24). He is not discussing any millennial kingdom of Christ. He is talking about an eternal state where death cannot exist. Therefore, he first makes the point that flesh and blood cannot inherit the kingdom because flesh and blood is subject to death and corruption. The human body must be changed and adapted to the eternal. This is obviously not preparation for a millennial kingdom, for even the premillennialists believe flesh and blood will inherit that kingdom; also death, though slowed down, will continue.

Paul reveals that the change that will be necessary prior to life in the eternal kingdom may take place in one of two ways. Those believers who die before the Lord comes will be changed by a resurrection, while those believers who are alive when the Lord comes will be changed, not by a resurrection, but by transformation. In other words, everybody will not die, but everybody will be changed before entering the final state. Even the souls that Christ brings with Him will need a body to house the spirit before they are in a complete or final state.

The writer next talks about the speed of the transformation. It will happen faster than one can bat an eye. It does not take God long to bring about the needed change. How different this is from the dispensational concept whereby God changes some pretribulation saints, and after 1,000 years He changes those who were saved above during the millennium. The bat of an eye is therefore scattered over at least 1,007 years; that is slow motion indeed. Even historic premillennialists scatter it over 1,000 years.

Paul also specifies the time of the needed change by saying it would happen at the "last trump" (v.51). Now, there is not any trumpet after the last trumpet; when the Lord sounds the last trumpet, everything as we know it will end. To claim that this last trumpet is only the last in a series and not necessarily the last trumpet is indeed a weak argument. The "last trumpet" is no doubt the same trumpet as the one spoken of in 1 Thessalonians 4:16, although the word "last" is not found in that account. Neither are the living saints said to be changed in the Thessalonian account; they are simply "caught up" (4:17). That does not mean they will not be changed; it only means Paul omitted saying so at that time. They will have to be transformed form flesh and blood before they can inherit the eternal kingdom rather than a millennial kingdom.

Paul actually follows this with an added thought. When the transformation happens, "Death is swallowed up in victory" (1 Cor. 15:54). When is this last enemy, death, to be destroyed? The writer has already answered that question when he said, "the LAST enemy that shall be destroyed is death" (1 Cor. 15:26).

What has Paul taught when the whole context of 1 Corinthians 15 is considered? He has taught us that there will be a resurrection and/or transformation of all believers. This will happen at the Second Coming of the Lord, as suddenly as the bat of an eye, at the sound of the last trumpet, and at the time death is destroyed. After the righteous are changed, there is no trumpet or death left.

Premillennialists, however, frequently tell us that there will be other trumpets and that death will continue during a tribulation period, a millennium, and during Satan's "little season" (Rev. 20:3,7-9).

In truth, 1 Corinthians 15:50-52 is used incorrectly by premillennialists who try to prove that the resurrection of the righteous is separated from the resurrection of the unrighteous by at least 1,000 years; it lends no real support to that argument. On the other hand, the passage conflicts in several ways with millennial thought. The resurrection of the unrighteous is not excluded by Paul's Corinthian account; it is, however, outside his purpose to discuss it.

The Resurrection and the Millennium

Revelation 20:4-6

Since Revelation 20 is the heart of premillennialism, it deserves to be discussed at length in a chapter of its own. Because this will be done later and because much repetition is not desirable, it is necessary to deal only briefly with Revelation 20:4-6 at this point. General concepts will be given, but most proof must await the chapter on Revelation 20. The passage in question reads as follows:

And I saw thrones, and they sat upon them, and judgment was given unto them: and I saw the souls of them that were beheaded for the witness of Jesus, and for the word of God, and which had not worshipped the beast, neither his image, neither had received his mark upon their foreheads, or in their hands; and they lived and reigned with Christ a thousand years. But the rest of the dead lived not again until the thousand years were finished. This is the first resurrection: blessed and holy is he that hath part in the first resurrection: on such the second death hath no power, but they shall be priests of God and of Christ, and shall reign with him a thousand years (Rev. 20:4-6).

In some ways this single passage says far too little about the millennium and in other ways far too much to please premillennialists. Since it is the only place in the Bible where the millennium is mentioned, is it not strange that it omits most of the extensive system of premillennial thought?

It is the opinion of this writer that revelation 20:4-6 should not be used as a primary proof text for premillennialism, but since it is the only place where a millennium of any type is mentioned, it is natural for all millennial arguments to start here. There are many reason why its use as a primary proof text is questionable. The following is a partial list of those reasons:

1) The language of this passage and book in general is filled with symbolic language, not clear and plain language. The symbolic should be interpreted by the clear and plain passages, not vice versa. For example, is the beast (v.4) an animal? Is the chain (v.1) used to bind Satan a literal chain? If not, why must the thousand years be interpreted as an exact time period?

2) It is difficult to be sure about a time sequence since the world ends several times in the Book of Revelation. Therefore, chapter 20 does not necessarily follow chapter 19 in time.

3) According to dispensationalists, the restoration of Israel accompanied by a literal fulfillment of Old Testament promises to Jews is the main purpose of the millennium: yet nothing is said in the passage about Jews, Palestine, the nation of Israel, a temple, animal sacrifices, Old Testament covenants etc.

4) The Jews are supposed to reign over Gentile nations and force Gentile nations to serve them, but John says nothing about this. Nevertheless, Lewis S. Chafer says, "It will be the time of Israel's glory and with Israel, some of the Gentiles will be blessed (Isa. 11:10; Matt. 25:34); but Gentiles must serve Israel"[2] (Isa. 14:1, 2; 60:12; 61:5).

5) The "beast" (v.4) is supposed to slaughter people during a future seven-year tribulation period, and those killed are to be rewarded by reigning with Christ during an earthly millennium. Dispensationalists, however, teach that the church will be raptured prior to the tribulation which would cause them to be rewarded for something they did not do, that is, if they participate in the millennium. If, on the other hand, this reward is confined to living tribulation saints, then the millennium will be very limited.

6) Dispensationalists insist on the one hand that the "first resurrection" (vv. 5, 6) is a bodily resurrection, and on the other hand they say the millennium is not for resurrected people. To say the least this is confusing. The passage says nothing about unresurrected persons, so if they participate they are not mentioned.

7) The place of the millennium is not earth but Heaven.

8) Those in the millennium are said to be in "soul" form, not bodily form.

9) The "first resurrection" is spiritual, beginning with regeneration and culminating in being raised to Heaven to reign with Christ in "soul" form. The prodigal son is an example of the first resurrection, for it was said of him, "For this my son was dead, and is alive again…" (Lk. 15:24). The dead who do not first reign with Christ in soul form will not reign with Him in bodily form at the second or bodily resurrection.

10) The first resurrection is contrasted with the second death (v.6);

The second death is not literal or physical, so why should the first resurrection have to be physical?

Chapter Summary

The chief passages dealing with the resurrection have now been examined. Three passages were found that placed the resurrection of the righteous and the unrighteous together (Dan. 12:2; Jn. 5:28,29; Acts 24:15). Not a single passage examined proved otherwise. While sometimes the resurrection of the unrighteous is not mentioned, that does not prove it is excluded. At times it did not fit the purpose of Biblical writers to deal with the resurrection of the wicked.

The strongest passage favoring the concept of the righteous being resurrected a millennium before the wicked is perhaps Revelation 20:4-6. There is no proof, however, that the "first resurrection" is the bodily resurrection of the righteous while the second resurrection is the bodily resurrection of the unrighteous. Internal evidence indicates that the "first resurrection" was not a bodily resurrection at all, but a spiritual resurrection beginning with regeneration and culminating in the "soul" (not body) reigning in Heaven with Christ.

If the Bible teaches a general resurrection, and we have given proof that it does, then it ought to teach a general judgment also; this is the subject of the next chapter.

Chapter 9

Prophecy and Judgment

The main purpose of this chapter is to determine if the Bible teaches one general judgment of both the living and the dead (whether believers or unbelievers), or if it teaches a series of judgments separated in time. Postmillennialists and amillennialists maintain that the Bible teaches a general universal judgment which will take place at the coming of the Lord and at the resurrection of the dead.

Premillennialists maintain that there will be a series of judgments separated in time, but they do not agree on the number of judgments. Dispensationalists often proclaim a larger number than other premillennialists. The Scofield Bible lists seven judgments as follows:

1) The Judgment of Believer's Sins
2) The Judgment of Self in the Believer
3) The Judgment of Believer's Works
4) The Judgment of Living Nations
5) The Judgment of Israel
6) The Judgment of Fallen Angels
7) The Great White Throne Judgment

While the Scofield Bible is generally considered the standard for dispensationalists, some reduce the number of judgments to either four or five. It is easy to drop the first two judgments in the list because they have nothing to do with eschatology. The big question then is, are the last five listed really different judgments separated by intervals of time, or is there only one judgment prophesied in different terminology? Premillennialists are united in the concept of multiple judgments, but the unity ends there. Different writers not only have a different number of judgments, but different names and descriptions also. The great variety in the premillennial presentation itself indicates a lack of clear Scriptural proof.

We will discuss the entire series of judgments outlined in the Scofield Bible while acknowledging that all premillennialists do not believe in all seven of those listed.

The Judgment of Believers' Sins

The dispensational series of judgments begin with The Judgment of Believers' Sins. It is claimed that this judgment took place approximately 2,000 years ago when Christ took our sins upon Himself and paid the penalty for them. Postmillennialists and amillennialists agree that Christ paid for our sins through his death on the cross but question that being called a judgment. For example, Boettner wrote, "But since no individuals appear in that transaction it is difficult to see on what grounds it should be called a judgment. Christ's work on the cross is more accurately referred to as an expiation or an atonement."[1] If the purpose of referring to this as a judgment is to establish the idea that there is more than one judgment, it is a weak argument, for it has nothing to do with eschatology.

The Judgment of Self in the Believer

Scofield's second judgment is called The Judgment of Self in the Believer. This so-called judgment is a continuous process in the life of every regenerated person. A person begins the process of self-examination at conversion and in the light of God's Word continues the process throughout life. In other words, the believer judges himself by God's Word throughout His life. Since this is a lifelong process of every believer, there is no reason to place it in the same classification as that of the final judgment. To do so only confuses people since it has nothing to do with eschatology and man's judgment at the coming of the Lord.

The Judgment of Believers' Works

The Judgment of Believers' Works is most often based upon the writings of Paul. He wrote:

For we must all appear before the judgment seat of Christ; that every one may receive the things done in his body, according to that he hath done, whether it be good or bad. Knowing therefore the terror of the Lord, we persuade men...(2 Cor. 5:10,11).

There is nothing in these verses to indicate that Paul is speaking of anything that is not part of the general judgment. To claim that the judgment here spoken of is 1,000 or 1,007 years before the judgment of Revelation 20:11-15 is to make a claim that the writer did not make. It is true that the Greek word for judgment seat is different in the two passages. In the first the Greek word is *Bema*, while in the latter it is *Thronos*. They have the same basic meaning except that in Acts 12:21 the word *Bematos* is translated throne. It reads, "And upon a set day Herod, arrayed in royal apparel, sat upon his throne, and made an oration unto them" (Acts 12:21). Therefore, the use of two separate words for judgment seat in no way warrants the idea of two different judgments.

The words, "We must all appear before the judgment seat of Christ" are said to be proof that only Christians are present at this judgment. Paul includes himself in the "we" and therefore, only Christians are included. Technically Old Testament saints are therefore ruled out also. This is a weak argument. It is called the judgment seat of Christ because Christ is the judge. It is true that he is telling Christians that they are going to be judged, but that does not mean the judgment is exclusively for them. It is simply the primary purpose of Paul on this occasion to speak to Christians concerning their being judged. The Christian will be held responsible for every idle word that he/she has spoken (Matt. 12:36, 37). A number of Scriptures teach a general judgment of all people. This passage (2. Cor. 5:10, 11) may deal primarily with Christians, but that does not mean that the judgment is exclusively Christian; it simply deals primarily with a part of the general judgment.

The Judgment of 2 Corinthians 5:10 is the same as the one described in Revelation 20. There it says:

And I saw the dead, small and great, stand before God; and the books were opened: and another book was opened, which is the book of life: and the dead were judged out of those things which were written in the books, according to their works. And the sea gave up the dead which were in it; and death and hell delivered up the dead which were in them: and they were judged every man according to their works (Rev. 20:12,13).

The first passage says "all" and "every man" while the second passage says "every man"; together they no doubt refer to the judgment of all people at the same time. In one the emphasis may be upon the righteous and in the other the primary emphasis may be upon the wicked, but neither passage excludes the other. Second Corinthians 5:11 also speaks of "the terror of the Lord"; this terminology surely refers to the wicked standing before their judge.

We conclude, therefore, that The Judgment of Believers' Works is not a separate judgment confined to Christians only. It is a name that someone made up for 2 Corinthians 5:10 and sometimes Romans 14:10. While the writer of these passages may have been dealing mainly with the judgment of believers, he does not exclude others. The judgment of believers is a part of the general judgment pointed to throughout the New Testament. All will be at the judgment and that includes believers. For example, a state official might address a group of criminals and lecture then on respect for the law, but that would not mean non-criminals need not respect the law. It is equally true that everyone must respect the law, or they will be subject to punishment. To argue otherwise simply because the state official addressed only criminals would be foolish. The same principle should be applied when interpreting 2 Corinthians 5:10 and Romans 14:10.

The Judgment of Living Nations

The forth judgment according to Scofield's list is The Judgment of Living Nations. It is based primarily upon Matthew 25:31-46. The judgment described in 2 Thessalonians 1:7-10 and in Acts 17:31 is also sometimes made to apply to The Judgment of Living Nations. This judgment is very important to premillennialists since for them it determines who enters the millennial kingdom.

Matthew 25:31-46

The passage reads as follows:

When the Son of man shall come in his glory, and all the holy angels with him, then shall he sit upon the throne of his glory: And before him shall be gathered all nations: and he shall separate them one form another, as a shepherd divideth his sheep from the goats: And he shall set the sheep on his right hand, but the goats on the left. Then shall the King say unto them on his right hand, Come, ye blessed of my Father, inherit the kingdom prepared for you from the foundation of the world: For I was hungered, and ye gave me meat: I was thirsty, and ye gave me drink: I was a stranger, and ye took me in: Naked, and ye clothed me: I was sick, and ye visited me: I was in prison, and ye came unto me. Then shall the righteous answer him, saying, Lord, when saw we thee hungered, and fed thee? Or thirsty, and gave thee drink? When saw we thee a stranger, and took thee in? or naked, and clothed thee? Or when saw we thee sick, or in prison, and came unto thee? And the King shall answer and say unto them, verily I say unto you, Inasmuch as ye have done it unto of the least of these my brethren, ye have done it unto me. Then shall he say unto them on the left hand, Depart from me, ye cursed, into everlasting fire, prepared for the devil and his angels: for I was hungered, and ye gave me no meat: I was thirsty, and ye gave me no drink: I was a stranger, and ye took me not in: naked, and ye clothed me not: sick, and in prison, and ye visited me not. Then shall they also answer him saying, Lord, when saw we thee hungered, or athrist, or a stranger, or naked, or sick, or in prison, and did not minister unto thee? Then shall he answer them, saying, Verily I say unto you, Inasmuch as ye did it not to one of the least of these, ye did it not to me. And these shall go away into everlasting punishment: the righteous into life eternal.

When the dispensationalist reads this passage, he generally concludes that 1) only living nations are involved for there is no resurrection mentioned, 2) the judgment scene is earthly, 3) three separate groups are being judged – sheep, goats, and brethren, 4) the time is when the Lord returns to earth (this He does not do at the so-called rapture), 5) the judgment is based upon one's treatment of the Jews (brethren), and 6) the destination is Hell for the goats or goat nations.

Non-premillennialists hold that this passage is a description of the general judgment at which time all people will be judged and rewarded accordingly. At the one future coming of Christ, He will burn the world and then judge it (2 Pet. 3:10,12; Rev. 20:11). The dead will be raised and judged also (1 Thess. 4:16; Jn. 5:28,29; Dan. 12:2; Rev. 20:12), although this fact is not pointed out in Mathew 25:31-46. The judgment has reference to eternity, not a millennium (v. 46). The "brethren" referred to are not Jews but are either Christians or those who were companions in suffering with Christ. "Brethren" could not refer to Jews nationally because they are included in the judgment of "all nations" (v. 32). Furthermore, Christ refused to recognize that blood relatives were his brethren. His brethren were those who were doing the will of God (Matt. 12:46-50).

Several facts are established in Matthew 25:31-46:

1) The time. It is, "When the Son of man shall come in his glory, and all the holy angels with him, then shall he sit upon the throne of his glory" (v.31).

2) Who is to be judged? It says, "And before him shall be gathered all nations…" (v.32). It does not say all living nations but all nations, meaning the people of all nations.

Since the premillennial system of doctrine will not work with a general judgment, we are often told that this is not a judgment of individuals, but nations. Not all nations are included, however, since Israel is excluded and judged separately. It is Gentile nations who are judged according to their treatment of the Jews. For example, Richard T. Dunham – a dispensationalist – states that, "Before him shall be gathered all nations. This has no reference to individuals.

God means what he says. The subjects of this judgment are the Gentile nations. This is no general judgement."[2] It is true that God means what He says, but not necessarily what dispensationalists think He says. What God says must be interpreted.

The Bible says "all nations" are included in this judgment, but dispensationalists say all except Israel. What did Matthew mean when he referred to "all nations"? Three chapters later he used the same terminology in the Great Commission when he said, "Go ye therefore, and teach ALL NATIONS, baptizing them in the name of the Father, and of the Son, and of the Holy Ghost" (Matt. 28:19). What did Matthew mean by "all nations" in this verse? Do we baptize nations or individuals that compose nations? Did Matthew intend to exclude the Jews from the Great Commission? The answer is obvious, and Matthew surely meant the same when he described the coming judgment. It was a judgment of individuals who collectively formed nations. Does this not harmonize with the rest of the Bible? Since when does the Bible teach anywhere that a person's eternal state is determined by what nation he lives in? To maintain that a person's eternal destination is determined by how he has treated non-Christians Jews is not Biblical.

That individuals, and not nations as a whole, are under discussion is made clear by some of the things they are said to have done. How do nations as a whole visit the sick and those in prison (vv. 39,44)?

Furthermore, while the word "nations" (Greek) is a neuter noun, the pronoun (them) which follows is masculine and therefore can only refer to individuals. The verse reads, "And before him shall be gathered all nations [neuter]: and he shall separate them [masculine] one from another, as a shepherd divideth his sheep from the goats" (v. 32).

According to this passage all people are being judged. Some, the righteous, are described as sheep, while others, the unrighteous, are described as goats. They are separated, an analogy that fits what the shepherds did with those animals during the life of Christ on earth. Verse 46 proves that this judgment was not to determine if one would enter the millennium but eternity. It says "And these shall go away into everlasting punishment: but the righteous into life eternal" (Matt. 25:46).

3) The results of the judgment. The two groups, sheep and goats, will receive different destinies. The goats (lost) will be assigned to "everlasting fire" (vv. 41,46) while the sheep (saved) will receive "life eternal" or the eternal state (v. 46). There is no hint of a millennium for either group.

The dispensational interpretation leaves several questions unanswered. 1) Where else in the Bible does it teach that the eternal destiny of an individual is determined by what others in one's nation does? 2) Where will the rebellious nations come from that are to rebel against Christ at the end of the millennium (Rev. 20: 8,9)? The wicked nations are destroyed prior to the millennium (Matt. 25:41,46), the righteous are given eternal life (Matt. 25:46) which would involve not being able to have children (Matt. 22:30; Lk. 20:34-36), and no one is resurrected according to dispensationalists. Thus where do all the rebellious people come from who are to be ruled with a rod of iron? The usual answer is that it will happen through children who are born during the millennium, but this would mean people who have been given eternal life will birth children. These "sheep" surely already had eternal life in the sense of salvation before the judgment or else salvation would be obtained at the judgment. The "life eternal" (v.46) therefore must refer to eternal life in either a resurrected or transformed state when Christians receive glorified bodies. 3) Why does "all nations" (v. 32) exempt Israel? 4) How can nations visit people in prison? It is obvious that they cannot. 5) If any nation is condemned to "everlasting fire" (v. 41), how could any individual in that nation escape that fire? 6) How is it that Gentiles can be granted eternal life on the basis of their relationship to the Jews when Jesus had already condemned the Jews in a series of woes (Matt. 23)? 7) How could all the people of the world be judged in "the Valley of Jehoshaphat) (Joel 3:2) which is a small ravine separating Jerusalem from the Mount of Olives? Remember that according to dispensationalists, we are talking about physical people; they say there are no resurrected people in the judgment of Matthew 25. Joel 3:2 was actually fulfilled long ago and has nothing to do with Matthew 25. Many unanswered questions, therefore, result from the premillennial assumption of several different judgment.

2 Thessalonians 1:7-10

And to you who are troubled rest with us, when the Lord Jesus shall be revealed from heaven with his mighty angels, In flaming fire taking vengeance on them that know not God, and that obey not the gospel of our Lord Jesus Christ: Who shall be punished with everlasting destruction from the presence of the Lord, and from the glory of his power; When he shall come to be glorified in his saints, and to be admired in all then that believe…. (2 Thess. 1:7-10).

Most premillennialists identify the judgment of this passage with the one described in Matthew 25:31-46. There are several similarities. It takes place at the coming of Christ; angels are present; both believers and non-believers are dealt with; and no specific point is made concerning a resurrection. It does not fit the pretribulation rapture concept because the wicked are judged and given eternal punishment. Neither does it fit the usual premillennial concept of the judgment described in Revelation 20:11-15 because they maintain that only lost people are dealt with at that judgment. They say who gets into the millennium is therefore settled at this judgment; this they believe is also true of Matthew 25:31-46.

The premillennial interpretation again leaves several questions unanswered. 1) How were the Thessalonian Christians then suffering for the kingdom of God (v. 5) when that kingdom according to premillennialism is yet to be established? This is suffering for something that does not exist. 2) How are those who had persecuted the Thessalonians Christians going to be punished with everlasting destruction when the Lord comes if they continue to sleep in the dust of the earth for another thousand years? 3) If it is claimed that they are to be RULED BY CHRIST with a rod of iron during the millennium, how is this classified as "everlasting destruction from the presence of the Lord" (v.9)? 4) how is it that when the Lord comes to be glorified in His saints (vv.7,10), He at the same time punishes those who have rejected Him, while pretribulationists claim He is glorified in His saints prior to a tribulation period but deals with the lost at a judgment following the millennium (Rev. 20:11-15)?

It makes more sense to see the events in 2 Thessalonians 1:7-10 as a single event or one description of the general judgment. The saints receive rest (v.7), Christ is revealed (v.7), the vengeance of Christ is demonstrated (v.8), the lost received eternal punishment (v.9), and the saints are glorified (v. 10). Non-premillennialists agree that this is the same judgment as that described in Matthew 25:31-46 but maintain that it is also the same judgment as Revelation 20:11-15; 2 Corinthians 5:10; etc. Second Thessalonians 1:7-10 is simply one description of the general judgment.

Acts 17:31

The Word of God declares:

Because he hath appointed a day, in the which he will judge the world in righteousness by that man whom he hath ordained; whereof he hath given assurances unto all men, in that he hath raised him from the dead (Acts 17:31).

Since it is said that Christ will "judge the world," not simply part of it, premillennialists again generally identify this Scriptural passage with Matthew 25:31-46 and 2 Thessalonians 1:7-10.

Non-premillennialists agree that Acts 17:31 is to be identified with Matthew 25:31-46 and 2 Thessalonians 1:7-10, but disagree that it should be limited to a relation with these judgment passages alone. There is no hint in Acts 17:31 that the judgment (singular) which is spoken of is one in a series. The language is the normal Biblical language which speaks of a general judgment without any identification with one in a series. If there were to be several different judgments, the Biblical writers should have known it and identified the judgment to which they were referring. They, however, never do this but speak of the judgment as a single event.

The Judgment of Israel

The fifth judgment in the dispensational scheme consists of a separate judgment for Israelites. Accordingly, God has a separate purpose for Israel and the church and must deal with them as two distinct bodies. They maintain that the Gentile nations will be judged according to their treatment of the Jews in the so-called Judgment of Living Nations. When speaking of The Judgment of Israel, Chafer wrote:

Quite in contrast to the experience accorded the Church (cf. John 5:24) the nation Israel must be judged, and it is reasonable to believe that this judgment will include all of that nation who in the past dispensations have lived under the covenants and promises. Therefore a resurrection of those generations of Israel is called for and must precede their judgment.[3]

When asked for Scripture to support the idea of a separate judgment of Israel, an Old Testament passage from Ezekiel is sometimes quoted. Ezekiel states:

As I live, saith the Lord GOD, surely with a mighty hand, and with a stretched out arm, and with fury poured out, will I rule over you: And I will bring you out from the people, and will gather you of the countries wherein ye are scattered, with a mighty hand, and with a stretched out arm, and with fury poured out. And I will bring you into the wilderness of the people, and there will I plead with you face to face. Like as I pleaded with your fathers in the wilderness of the land of Egypt, so will I plead with you, saith the Lord GOD. And I will cause you to pass under the rod, and I will bring you into the bond of the covenant: And I will purge out from among you the rebels, and them that transgress against me: I will bring them forth out of the country where they sojourn, and they shall not enter into the land of Israel: and ye shall know that I am the LORD (Ezek. 20:33-38).

Of course Israel is dealt with in this passage, for she was God's chosen nation during the Old Testament period. God did see that a remnant of Jews returned after captivity. There is, however, no proof that this passage was intended to prove that a separate and yet future judgment for Israel will occur just prior to an earthly millennium. Such proof is needed but wholly lacking. The word judgment is not even used in the passage, but God did promise to bring Israel "under the rod" (v. 37) before she was allowed to return from Babylonian captivity. The New Testament message concerning the judgment is that all will be judged and that includes Israel.

The Judgment of Fallen Angels

Scofield's sixth judgment is called The Judgment of Fallen Angels. Satan is generally identified with these fallen angels. Peter says, "For if God spared not the angels that sinned, but cast them down to hell, and delivered them into chains of darkness, to be preserved unto judgment" (2 Pet. 2:4). Paul states: "Know ye not that we shall judge angles"? (1 Cor. 6:3). Jude adds, "And the angels which kept not their first estate, but left their own habitation, he hath reserved in everlasting chains under darkness unto THE JUDGMENT OF THE GREAT DAY" (Jude 6).

These passages do not suggest a long drawn out judgment that is separate from the Day of Judgment for the human race. Nevertheless, Lewis S. Chafer says, "Having conquered the nations at the time of His return to the earth Christ will then undertake the stupendous task of subduing angelic powers, and this will be extended over His entire millennial reign."[4] It is odd theology that makes Christ so weak that it will take him a thousand years to subdue one portion of His creation. The resurrected Christ Himself said, "All power is given unto me in heaven and in earth" (Matt. 28:18). There is absolutely no Scriptural proof that the judgment of angels is on a separate day or at a separate time from the general judgment day.

The Great White Throne Judgement

Scofield calls his seventh and final judgment The Great White Throne Judgment, a name taken from Revelation 20:11. The entire judgment passage reads as follows:

And I saw a great white throne, and him that sat on it, from whose face the earth and the heaven fled away; and there was found no place for them. And I saw the dead, small and great, stand before God: and the books were opened: and another book was opened, which is the book of life: and the dead were judged out of those things which were written in the books, according to their works. And the sea gave up the dead which were in it; and death and hell delivered up the dead which were in them: and they were judged every man according to their works. And death and hell were cast into the lake of fire. This is the second death. And whosoever was not found written in the book of life was cast into the lake of fire (Rev. 20:11-15).

The usual premillennial explanation of this passage is that it is a judgment exclusively for the wicked with no righteous people present. This of course would make it different from the judgment of nations (Matt. 25:31-46). Dr. Lewis Chafer states it concisely by saying, "At the judgment of the nation's three classes are present – 'sheep', 'goats,' and Christ's 'brethren,' – while at the judgment of the great white throne there is but one class – the wicked dead."[5]

The dispensational position is incorrect for two reasons. First, Christ's "brethren" of Matthew 25:40 should be considered "sheep" rather than a third class. Every person is either saved or lost, a sheep or a goat. There are, therefore, only two broad classes of people. This harmonizes with Scripture in general. Second, both classes are present at the great white throne judgment of Revelation 20:11-15.

Notice that the passage begins with the expression, "And I saw the dead, small and great…" (v.12). The passage does not say the wicked dead or part of the dead. That may be what some want it to say, but it declares that "the dead" are seen; and unless the writer qualifies his statement, that expression should mean all the dead. John no doubt meant the same as was given in his gospel account when it was said:

Marvel not at this" for the hour is coming, in the which ALL that were in the graves shall hear his voice, And shall come forth; they that have done good, unto resurrection of life; and they that have done evil, unto the resurrection of damnation (Jn. 5:28,29).

The expression "small and great" (v. 12) could very well refer to both the righteous and the wicked. Other Scriptural passages teach that all will stand before the judgment seat of God (Matt. 16:27; 25:32; Rom. 14:10; 2 cor. 5:10; 2 Tim. 4:1; Heb. 9:27).

Not only were books opened at this judgment which contained the deeds of the wicked, but "another book was opened, which is the book of life" (v.12). Then "the dead" (not part of the dead) were judged out of whatever books were appropriate. If this judgment concerned the wicked only, there would be no need for the book of life to be opened and people judged out of it.

The passage further states that "every man," meaning every person, was judged (v.13). Some were then condemned and cast into the "lake of fire) (v.14). John declares that "whosoever was not found written in the book of life was cast into the lake of fire" (v. 15). This clearly implies that some were found written in the book of life, but those who were not end up in the lake of fire.

The expression "the dead" is used four times in this passage, but in neither place is it limited to part of the dead. The "book of life" is referred to twice in the passage, but there is no need for the presence of the book of life if the righteous are not present. The passage does not hint that the righteous have already been judged. On the other hand, it strongly implies that the dead of all ages are present. The general terminology of the whole passage implies that all the dead regardless of where they were, or who they were, would be at this judgment.

There is no Biblical reason to believe that John describes anything other than a general judgment which he had earlier spoken of in his gospel and which other Biblical writers spoke of for their own purpose and in their own language. It is admitted that the righteous will not be condemned, but they will be judged, vindicated, and rewarded. Condemnation is not the only purpose of judgment. Finally, it would have been pointless for the writer of Revelation to conclude by saying, "And whosoever was not found written in the book of life was cast into the lake of fire" (v.15), if no one's name was found written in the book of life.

Other Judgment Passages

The seven so-called separate judgments with their various Scriptures have now been discussed. There are, however, several other passages concerning the judgment which should be considered.

1) First, there are the general resurrection Scriptures which definitely imply a judgment of all at the same time – Daniel 12:2; John 5:28, 29; and Acts 24:15. Daniel speaks of some awaking to everlasting life while other awake to shame and everlasting contempt. Will this happen without a general judgment? John speaks of all coming out of the grave at the same hour; some to the resurrection of life and others to the resurrection of damnation. Will this happen without a general judgment? Paul, who is quoted by Luke in Acts 24:15, said there would be a resurrection of the dead, both of the just and the unjust. Will it be determined who is just and who is unjust without a general judgment? The answer is obviously no. General resurrection Scriptures imply a general judgment.

2) Second, there is the parable of the wheat and tares found in Matthew 13:24:43. The meaning of the parables may sometimes be questionable but not so in this case; Jesus interpreted this parable for us. He clearly taught that all, whether classified as wheat or tares, would be judged. He further taught that there would be no separation of these two classes until the harvest at the end of the world. A pretribulation rapture would not be the end of the world. Jesus then taught the same truth through the parable of the net used by fishermen (vv.47-50).

3) Third, there is the conclusion to the book of Ecclesiastes. There the writer says:

Let us hear the conclusion of the whole matter: Fear God, and keep his commandment: for this is the whole duty of man. For God shall bring every work into judgment, with every secret thing, whether it be good, or whether it be evil (Ecc. 12:13,14).

The writer does not suggest that there will be a judgment for the "good" at one time period and then much later a judgment for the "evil." The passage simply teaches that every work that every person has done will have to be accounted for in some way at the judgment.

4) Above all, the words of Jesus should be considered. He said "For the Son of man shall come in the glory of his Father with his angels; and THEN he shall reward EVERY MAN according to his works" (Matt. 16:27). If Jesus told us the truth, and He did, He will reward every person, not just the righteous, at His coming. This is in accord with Scriptures in general.

5) Those Scriptures which proclaim that the judgment will consist of both the quick (living) and the dead should also be considered. It is stated in Acts, "And he commanded us to preach unto the people, and to testify that it is he which was ordained of God to be the Judge of quick and dead" (Acts 10:42). Paul said, "I charge thee therefore before God, and the Lord Jesus Christ, who shall judge the quick and the dead at his appearing and his kingdom" (2 Tim. 4:1). Peter states it thusly, "Who shall give account to him that is ready to judge the quick and the dead" (1 Pet. 4:5). These three passages teach that the Lord will judge at His appearing both the quick (living) and the dead. If occasionally a writer refers to the judgment and does not

mention both groups that does not mean that both will not be present. It only means that it was outside the purpose of the writer to mention both at the time.

Chapter Summary

We conclude that the doctrine of a series of judgments is not based upon Biblical authority but upon the need for those advocating dispensationalism. Multiple judgments and resurrections results from an incorrect interpretation of Revelation 20:4-6. A faulty interpretation of Revelation 20 will force one to retrace his steps through the whole Bible and reinterpreted all resurrection and judgment passages. This in turn causes many clear Biblical statements to be reinterpreted to harmonize with a preconceived idea of what is taught in the symbolic passage of Revelation 20:4-6. Symbolical passages should be interpreted to agree with the clear and plain passages, and not vice versa. It is therefore necessary to discuss Revelation 20 at this time.

Chapter 10

Prophecy and Revelation 20

We have now arrived at Revelation 20, the so-called keystone of prophecy. This single passage is so important to premillennialists that they are willing to retrace their steps back through the entire Bible and reinterpret it in the light of what they think this passage teaches. All Scriptures concerning Israel, the resurrection, the judgement, etc. must now be reevaluated in the light of this passage. This seems wrong, but before proceeding with this thought and the interpretation of Revelation 20, it is necessary to first think of Revelation as a whole.

For a thorough understanding of Revelation with its apocalyptic form and presentation of the five major methods of interpreting the book, the reader may examine *Worthy Is The Lamb* by the Southern Baptist theologian – Ray Summers. Homer Hailey, in *Revelation; An Introduction and Commentary,* also covers well these five major methods of interpretation – futurist, continuous-historical, philosophy of history, preterits, and historical-background. Both of these authors favor the historical-background method, and both works are listed in the bibliography of this book. It is not within the purpose of this work to deal extensively with Revelation as a whole; that is left to others.

In *More Than Conquers*, William Hendriksen also makes a major contribution to the interpretation of Revelation. He is by no means the only author to explain the concept of parallelism or progressive parallelism found in revelation, but he is a well-recognized one. According to parallelism the basic outline of Revelation is somewhat as follows: 1) Chapters 1-3 – the story of John's vision of the resurrected Christ and His message to the seven churches of Asia are told. It covers the whole span of time between the first and second coming of Christ. 2) Chapters 4-7 – under a vision of Seven Seals the entire gospel age is pictured from the Roman Empire to the end with a reference to the final judgment (6:12-17; 7:9-17). 3) Chapters 8-11 – under a vision of Seven Trumpets the same entire gospel age is pictured with a reference near the end to the final judgment and to the end of time as we know it (11:15,18). 4) Chapters 12-14 – under a vision of a woman and the man-child the time between Christ's birth and Second Coming is surveyed (12:5; 14:14-20). 5) Chapters 15,16 – under the vision of Seven Bowls of Wrath the gospel age is again surveyed to its end (16:20). 6) Chapters 17-19 – under a vision of the Great Harlot and the Beasts, history is traced to its end (19:11). 7) Chapters 20-22 – in chapter 20 we again start over in time and are introduced to the binding of Satan in a restrictive way (he can no longer keep nations from truth nor maintain emperor worship) which was accomplished by Christ's first coming. Christ's Second Coming and Satan's ultimate doom are then foretold and the judgment predicted. In chapters 21 and 22 we go beyond the judgment and end of this age. Eternity is introduced; this is not simply parallelism but progressive parallelism; that is, we are taken beyond our previous point.

Note that according to this view, the Book of Revelation has seven sections which run somewhat parallel to each other. Each section, under a different symbol, depicts good and evil from the first advent of Christ to the time of His Second Coming. This, of course, differs greatly from the concept that what happens in one chapter always follows that which happened in the preceding chapter. Parallelism rather than chronological order is John's method of writing.

Time will not presently permit an extensive presentation of parallelism as found in Revelation. This is left to those with complete works on the Book of Revelation.

Revelation as a Whole

There are, however, a few basic premises that should be understood concerning the Book of Revelation.

1) Revelation is apocalyptic literature.

Revelation admittedly is a book with figures of speech, poetic language, symbols, numerology, and spiritual truths veiled in Old Testament terminology. While the figures, symbols, etc. are not real, they do represent that which is real. Modern society generally is not accustomed to such literature; it desires plain or literal language. But to understand Revelation, one must learn to think in terms of the society of John's day. Its first, but not exclusive, application must be made to that society.

Much of the language in Revelation is obviously not intended to be literalized; spiritual truths must be sought. For example, it portrays fire-breathing horses that kill with the sting of their tails, a dragon whose tail can knock a third of the stars out of the sky, multiple-headed beasts, and frogs that come out of the mouth of a dragon. The list is almost endless.

Apocalyptic literature was normal among Jews, especially during periods of danger. This was true during the Old Testament economy as well. When Christ was threatened with death before His time to die, He often turned to figurative language and parables. Those who sought to crucify Him were frustrated and asked Him to tell them in plain language if He were the promised Messiah. His predictions concerning His death and resurrection were veiled in figurative language. He spoke of people needing to be born again and of the necessity to eat His flesh and drink His blood. It is, therefore, not strange that He would reveal truth through figurative language to His servant – John. It enabled John to proclaim truth in such a way that his generation could understand it and at the same time be relatively safe from Roman prosecutors.

To make Revelation, as futurists do, apply exclusively to what is yet a future generation is wrong. John did not try to comfort the persecuted of his day by proclaiming that life would get easier within a few thousand years.

2) The symbols of Revelation cannot be interpreted literally.

In spite of premillennialists' claims concerning interpreting the Book of Revelation literally, no one (dispensationalists included) does so; in fact, no one even comes close. All interpret revelation figuratively; it is only a matter of when or where one decides to interpret figuratively or literally. Proof of this will be given later in the interpretation of Revelation 20.

3) Biblical books written in figurative language should be interpreted figuratively unless there are indications to do otherwise.

In apocalyptic literature, those who think literally will miss the intended message. Because Old Testament prophecy was over-literalized by the people of Christ's day, many of them did not recognize Christ as their promised king and Messiah. The Jews paid a great price for this over-literalizing and people of today will do the same.

4) Obscure passages of Scripture must be interpreted by the clear and plain, not vice versa.

This is a generally accepted rule of hermeneutics. To reinterpret the rest of the Bible that is written in clear and plain language by an obscure passage such as Revelation 20:1-6 is a clear violation of this rule. Revelation 20 should be interpreted by all that goes before it, not vice versa. Since Revelation 20 is couched in symbolic, not plain language, it should not be thought of as the keystone of Biblical prophecy. One can prove almost anything in the Book of Revelation by manipulating the symbols found therein.

5) Persecution of Christians was severe when Revelation was written.

At the time of the writing of Revelation, Domitian was probably the emperor of the Roman Empire, and emperor worship was the law of the land. Christians claimed a higher citizenship and refused emperor worship; this sometimes led to their death. Christians were considered fanatic traitors. John, the author of Revelation, was banished to the Isle of Patmos and according to tradition, was the only apostle who died a natural death. It should not amaze us that he would refer to an emperor as a beast rather than call his name. Naming names could be hazardous to one's health. Furthermore, it was not necessary; the message could be understood by his generation through symbolic language.

6) The purpose of Revelation was to reveal through symbols the conflict between good and evil and the results of that conflict.

While the symbols of Revelation were not real, they represented something that was. The conflict raged and although it may not have always appeared so, Christ was on His throne and in control. The message was that Christians should remain faithful regardless of the severity of the evil forces. That was not only true when Revelation was written, but it is still true today. The faithful few will succeed in all ages, not by dodging persecution, but in spite of it. True Christians will be persecuted today if they have the courage to speak out on modern issues such as secular humanism, sex outside of marriage, homosexuality, the legalizing of abortion, pornography, alcohol, gambling, prostitution, etc. The only way to remain popular with the world is to pay the bill for the teaching of secular humanism, support any desired Christian enterprise privately, and remain silent concerning anything the government desires to legalize and tax. The Roman government got upset with Christians when they did not obey what the state had legalized and so will modern governments. True Christians, however, have no choice but to advocate, in a kind way, the values of their master – Christ.

7) The theme of Revelation is Christian victory.

In Revelation the forces of evil may be pictured in many different ways – a beast, a false prophet, a dragon, or Satan himself – but victory ultimately lies with Christ and His followers. The forces of evil may do great harm and even appear victorious at times, but in the end Christians are the winners. In Revelation this even included those Christians who lost their lives. Christ is pictured as conquering the beast, the false prophet, the dragon, Satan, Hell, and the grave. Furthermore, Revelation pictures Christians reigning in Heaven for a symbolic thousand years (20:4), and after receiving a new body as dwelling eternally in a new Heaven and earth (22:5). The clear message is that Christians are winners; this is much more important than the ability to identify whom a beast, etc. symbolizes.

While keeping these introductory concepts in mind, it is now time to examine Revelation 20 itself. The chapter divides itself naturally into four divisions. These divisions will be discussed chronologically.

The Binding of Satan on Earth

Rev. 20:1-3

And I saw an angel come down from heaven, having the key of the bottomless pit and a great chain in his hand. And he laid hold on the dragon, that old serpent, which is the Devil, and Satan, and bound him a thousand years, And cast him into the bottomless pit, and shut him up, and set a seal upon him, that he should deceive the nations no more, till the thousand years should be fulfilled: and after that he must be loosed a little season (Rev. 20:1-3).

Some things are obvious in Revelation 20:1-3. Undeniably the central thought is the binding of Satan, not the duration of that binding. It is also obvious that this binding of Satan is proclaimed by means of symbols. The principle millennial views will now be presented with their answers to eight questions concerning the binding of Satan. These questions are: 1) Who does the binding? 2) Where does the binding take place? 3) When did the binding take place? 4) What is the duration of the binding? 5) Where is the one bound placed? 6) What is the meaning of the binding? 7) What about the symbols used to describe the binding? And 8) What is meant by the loosing which follows the binding?

The Premillennial Response

Premillennialists believe the "angel" who does the binding will be Christ. The place of the binding will be the earth. The time of the binding is future; it will follow the Second Coming of Christ already reported in chapter 19. In other words, they maintain that Revelation is written chronologically, and what is found in chapter 20 naturally follows what is recorded in chapter 19. The person bound, Satan, will be shut up in a bottomless pit or abyss and sealed so that he cannot influence those who live during the thousand-year period. The binding means that he will be incapacitated and unable to spread his influence. Premillennialists generally agree that symbols such as the key, chain, bottomless pit, sealing, etc. are simply figures of speech. They also agree that Satan is not at one time both a dragon and a serpent; it is taken as poetic language. The loosing is the release of Satan from the abyss for a short period during which he will cause the world to rebel against Israel, the headquarters of the millennial kingdom.

Premillennialists are not agreed as to whether this will be near the end of the millennium or after it.

The Postmillennial Response

Postmillennialists generally agree that the "angel" who binds Satan is Christ and the place of the binding is the earth. They, however, do not believe that the binding is totally future. Postmillennialists maintain that Satan always has been restricted, was even more restricted as a result of the first advent of Christ, and that his binding is continuous. One postmillennialists – Loraine Boettner – wrote:

We must, therefore, reject the view that the binding of Satan referred to in Revelation 20:2 was accomplished by Christ's triumph over him at the cross. We hold rather that the binding of Satan is a process continuing through this dispensation as evil is more and more suppressed, as the world is more and more Christianized, and as there is therefore less and less occasions for God to use the Devil as an instrument in the punishing of sinners.[1]

As far as the question of duration is concerned, postmillennialists look upon the binding of Satan as a process rather than an act. The place of confinement and the bottomless pit, is not taken literally, and the restriction is not total or absolute. Satan still roams about as a roaring lion (1 Pet. 5:8) but will become more and more restricted as time passes. What is the meaning of the binding? Postmillennialists teach that in its first application the binding is not total but concerns Satan's ability to deceive the nations as he did in Old Testament times, a time when all nations except Israel were in darkness. However, their application does not stop with this; they believe Satan is being bound tighter and tighter as the chain (gospel) is being extended.

What about the symbols of Revelation 20:1-3? The language as a whole is taken as figurative in nature. Neither the key, the bottomless pit, the chain, the dragon, the serpent, the binding, the seal, nor the thousand years is taken literally. They are presented as something that represents the real. Finally, what is meant by the loosing? Postmillennialists generally teach that Satan's influence will increase for a short period just prior to the return of Christ. Only God knows the reason why Satan is allowed extra powers in the end-time.

The Amillennial Response

1) Who does the binding? Amillennialists generally agree with postmillennialists and premillennialists that the "angel" who does the binding is actually Christ. Christ did claim in the Book of Revelation itself that He had the keys to Hell and death (1:18). Other angels, including Michael the archangel, seemed unwilling to test Satan in some aspects (Jude 9). Furthermore, it is generally believed that Christ did appear to Abraham, Jacob, and Moses in the form of an angel. When all is considered, it seems logical to conclude that the "angel" is none other than Christ. A few amillennialists, however, disagree.

2) Where does the binding take place? Since the angel came down from Heaven to do the binding, it is only logical to conclude that it is an earthly binding. All three millennial camps generally agree on this item, but beyond this point agreement became scarcer.

3) When did the binding of Revelation 20:1-3 take place? The premillennialists say that it is future that it will happen only after the Second Coming of Christ. They maintain that the record of the return of Christ is found in

chapter 19 and the events of chapter 20 must follow chronologically. Amillennialists believe this doctrine is the result of a false assumption. The Second Coming of Christ may be indicated in chapter 19, but that does not necessarily mean that the events of chapter 20 must follow. John, the author, does not say that what he saw in chapter 20 followed what he saw in chapter 19; he merely revealed another vision. Some say that silence means we should take the events of the two chapters chronologically. But this is not necessarily true due to the nature of the Bible. The Old Testament has three sections (historical, poetical, and prophetical), and they are not chronological in nature. The nature of the literature rather than when it was written determined its location in the Scriptures. When one gets to the end of Nehemiah, the historical section, he is at the end of the Old Testament time-wise. All the rest of the Old Testament must be placed back into the time period covered in the historical division. In the New Testament one discovers quickly that the writers do not present chronologically the events in the life of Christ.

It has already been pointed out that chapters 20-22 comprise the last of seven parallel sections found in Revelation. They, therefore, do not start out describing what follows the events of chapter 19; instead, John starts over again and relates in a new way what happened when Christ came the first time and then proceeds through history.

Both the whole of the Bible and chapter 20 support this view. To say that Satan will be bound after the Second Coming of Christ, then released, contradicts the whole of Scripture. Scriptures generally picture this world ending when Christ comes the second time, a fact that has already been established in this book. But does Revelation 20 support this concept? Yes, look at the order of events. Satan is bound (1-3), saints reign in Heaven with Christ (4-6), Satan is loosed (7-10), and then Christ returns in fire to judge (9-15: cf. 2 Thess. 1:7-10). All, including Satan, are given their final destination. The judgment is everywhere pictured as taking place when Christ comes, not a thousand years later. The binding of Satan is therefore before the Second Coming of Christ, not after it; the events of chapter 20 do not follow chronologically the events of chapter 19.

Is there any Biblical evidence that the binding of Satan took place at Christ's first coming? The answer is yes. Christ, according to Matthew 12, claimed that He bound Satan. When Christ cast out demons (evil spirits or devils), the Pharisees claimed He did it through the prince of devils. Christ gave a logical rebuttal and then said:

But if I cast our devils by the Spirit of God, then the kingdom of God is come unto you. Or else how can one enter into a strong man's house, and spoil his goods, except he first BIND the strong man? And then he will spoil his house (Matt. 12:28,29).

It is clear that Christ here is teaching that He had to bind Satan before He could take his subjects. Satan could be bound or restricted before Christ's atonement just as Christ could forgive sins; His atonement at the time of the crucifixion, however, was the basis of that authority.

4) What is the duration of the binding? Premillennialists plead with us to take the Bible for what it says, and it plainly says a thousand years. If we do not believe that, then we are spiritualizing away Biblical truth. What shall we say? There is no real logic or Biblical authority for the premillennial claim. What about the logic of the argument? They admit that other symbols in the

passage are not real- the key, the chain, the seal, etc. They say they understand that one cannot bind a spirit being with a literal chain. Where is the logic then in demanding that the thousand years be taken literally when much of the rest of the same passage is taken symbolically?

Second, why should the expression "a thousand years" be taken as an exact number? It is not taken that way elsewhere in the Scriptures. A thousand years is the cube of ten and symbolizes vastness or a whole. The Lord said, "For every beast of the forest is mine, and the cattle upon a thousand hills" (Ps. 50:10). A thousand here simply implies vastness; it does not mean that God's ownership of cattle is limited to a thousand hills, for he actually owns all cattle on all hills. It is a figure of speech not to be taken literally; it stands for an indeterminate but complete number (see Duet. 1:10,11; Job 9:3; 33:23; Eccl. 6:6; 7:28). The expression "a thousand" is therefore not usually taken literally in the Bible and since it is among symbolic language in Revelation 20:1-3, it is herein maintained that it should not be taken literally.

The expression "a thousand years" in Revelation 20:1-3 is used as a figure of speech, and it covers the time period from the binding of Satan (Rev. 20:2) until the loosing of Satan (Rev. 20:7). Since Satan was bound at the first advent of Christ (Jn. 12:31) and will not be loosed until just prior to his Second Coming, the symbolic thousand years may be said to cover roughly the time period between Christ's first and second advent. This, of course, has already greatly exceeded a literal one thousand-year period, but it fits the way the expression is used elsewhere in the Scriptures. It should also be remembered here that there in Revelation 20 it is in the midst of symbolism.

5) Where is the bound person (Satan) placed? All agree on where this is. Amillennialists do not think of it as a literal hole in the earth with a lid on it. The passage as a whole indicates Satan is restricted but not totally confined. Proof that he is not being punished or totally confined is found in the fact that according to the account as a whole this happens to him when he is cast into the lake of fire and brimstone (v. 10). Until that time Satan is being bound in the sense of restriction. This binding is often likened to a vicious dog on a long chain; he can do a considerable amount of damage if one gets within his reach; nevertheless, he is confined, limited, or restricted. According to the Bible a woman is bound to her husband (Rom. 7:3), but that does not mean she is without liberty. The marriage contract is actually binding on both the husband and the wife, yet, they possess a lot of freedom. The bottomless pit is a figure of speech. Satan is not confined the same way as a person who is in jail; he still has access to all the earth.

6) What is the meaning of this binding? Is Satan unable to do anything? Premillennialists frequently picture Satan as being bound to the point that he has no influence during their anticipated earthly millennium. Does the passage before us indicated such a binding? No, the only restriction mentioned in the passage is found in the expression "that he should deceive the nations no more, till the thousand years should be fulfilled" (v. 3). But what does "deceive the nations" mean? Before the binding which took place when Christ came the first time, Satan was basically able to keep the truth from all nations except Israel. In Israel a small number of Jews plus a few proselytes received the truth even if they did not always obey it. Before the Lord left the earth, he gave the commission to His disciples to carry the gospel to the entire world. That process began

among Jews at Pentecost and soon spread to Gentile nations. Satan could not continue indefinitely his domination over John's society through Roman emperors with their demand for emperor worship. John told the persecuted Christians of his day about this binding of Satan; the process had actually already begun. This is what is meant by the binding of Satan; it was a partial binding. Revelation 20:1-3 is preventive in nature while the binding in Revelation 20:10 is punitive. The Abyss is not final but the lake of fire will be.

7)   What about the symbols used to describe the binding? Amillennialists do not believe the symbols are real, but that they do represent that which is real; Satan was bound but not with a material key, chain, seal, etc. Neither was he placed in a prison. Satan was referred to as both a serpent and a dragon; obviously these are figures of speech, for Satan is a spirit being. People should not necessarily get upset when someone says something in the Bible is figurative; figurative expressions stand for realities. For example, Jesus is referred to as the Lamb of God, and in this expression is found a great spiritual truth. It does not mean, however, that Christ is a four-legged animal. Symbolic language is not unusual in the Bible; to the contrary, it is rather normal. It was the non-biblical world that rarely used symbolism.

8)   What is meant by the loosing which follows the binding? This loosing of Satan causes both the earthly millennium of premillennialists and postmillennialists to end in failure. Premillennialists have Christ personally reigning for a thousand years, yet His reign ends in worldwide rebellion. Such an ending seems out of place. The earthly millennium of the postmillennialists is quite different in nature. Christ is not visible here, but He reigns in the hearts

of people to the point that most of the world is converted. When Satan is loosed, the effectiveness of Christ disappears. This seems strange too. The amillennialists do not have the same problem because the loosing of Satan does not affect their heavenly millennium; that millennium does not fail, for Satan cannot invade Heaven.

Amillennialists see reason to believe that we may have already entered the period of Satan's loosing. With the rise of communism, Satan appears to be regaining some nations. A few other non-communist nations are presently shutting the door to Christianity. Time will tell if this is the predicted loosing of Satan. By then, it may however, be too late for many. Amillennialists, contrary to premillennialists, do not believe any can be saved after Christ returns.

In summary, we have found that the period of Satan's binding, figuratively referred to as "a thousand years" of time, had a wonderful message for those of the earth who were dominated by emperors who demanded worship. The message was that such domination would soon end; Satan could not prevent it. Let us now look at the second division of Revelation 20. Here the scene changes from earth to Heaven and reveals how the victorious saints were faring.

The Reigning of Martyrs in Heaven

Rev. 20:4-6

And I saw thrones, and they sat upon them, and judgment was given unto them: and I saw the souls of them that were beheaded for the witness of Jesus, and for the word of God, and which had not worshipped the beast, neither his image, neither had received his mark upon their foreheads, or in their hands; and they lived and reigned with Christ a thousand years. But the rest of the dead lived not again until the thousand years were finished. This is the first resurrection. Blessed and holy is he that hath part in the first resurrection: on such the second death hath no power, but they shall be priests of God and of Christ, and shall reign with him a thousand years (Rev. 20:4-6).

While the binding of Satan was the theme of Revelation 20:1-3, this second division is concerned mainly with the reigning of Christian martyrs. The division will also be examined in the light of a series of questions. These questions are:

1) When does the millennium take place?
2) Who is in the millennium?
3) Where is the millennium?
4) What is meant by "judgment was given unto them?"
5) What is meant by "mark of the beast"?
6) What is the duration of the millennium?
7) What is meant by "rest of the dead"?
8) What is meant by "first resurrection"?
9) What is meant by "second death"?
10) What about the symbols used in describing the millennium?

The Premillennial Response

1) When does the millennium take place? Premillennialists contend that it will happen after the Second Coming of Christ and during the same period as the binding of Satan. It is, therefore, believed to be in the future.

2) Who is in the millennium? Premillennialists differ on this issue. Some say all Christians, while others maintain that only certain people who happen to be living; that is, there will be no resurrected people involved.

Accordingly, the living wicked will be destroyed, and the living righteous will enter the millennium.

3) Where is the millennium? All premillennialists maintain that it will be on earth and Jerusalem will be the capital. Any heavenly concept of a millennium is firmly rejected.

4) What is meant by "judgment was given unto them"? To the premillennialist this means that in the future millennium, saints will share in some way with Christ in ruling over and judging the nations. It is not believed to have anything to do with saints being judged themselves.

5) What is meant by "mark of the beast"? The beast is believed to be a future end-time ruler (antichrist) who will literally force his subjects to receive a mark of some kind that will identify them as loyal to him. Those who refuse the mark will probably be killed.

6) What is the duration of the millennium? It is believed to be a thousand years, no more and no less. "A thousand years" is a literal number, not a figure of speech.

7) What is mean by "rest of the dead"? Premillennialists say it is the wicked part of the dead who will be resurrected after the millennium; the resurrection of the righteous, called the first resurrection, will precede the millennium.

8) What is meant by "first resurrection"? All premillennialists believe it will be the bodily resurrection of the righteous; they do not, however, agree on when it will take place or if it will have more than one stage. For an explanation, please refer back to the chapter on the resurrection.

9) What is meant by "second death"? It is thought to be a second type of death; it will be eternal punishment for the wicked in a lake of fire (v. 10). It is not generally thought to be an end of existence. There is first physical death, but it will be followed by a second death of a spiritual nature and it will last forever.

10) What about the symbols used in describing the millennium? Premillennialists admit that some of the language is symbolic; nevertheless, they keep their interpretation largely literal. To be totally literal would mean "souls" could not be interpreted as people in the flesh, and the "beast" would have to be an animal, etc. Some premillennialists have to symbolize the word "beheaded" because they do not believe any who have died will be in the millennium. This passage, however, indicates otherwise.

While the position of premillennialists as it relates to the ten question has now been given, that is not the whole of the premillennial position. Premillennialists emphasize the importance of certain things to the millennium, such as the Jews, Palestine, Jerusalem, a throne in Jerusalem, a rebuilt Temple, the reinstatement of animal sacrifices, longevity of life, domestication of wild animals, increased productivity, a restoration of the Law of Moses, and the physical reign of Christ. In spite of this emphasis, the only account of the millennium, Revelation 20, does not mention any of these. Does this not seem strange?

The Postmillennial Response

1) When does the millennium take place? Postmillennialists say that it is before, not after, the Second Coming of Christ. To them the millennium is a result of world Christianization which will precede Christ's return.

Christ is not visible; He reigns in the hearts of His people, and they reign with Him in the evangelization process.

2) Who is in the millennium? All living upon the earth at that time who have Christ living in their hearts. There are no physically resurrected beings in the postmillennial millennium. Every physical saint lives with Christ, reigns with Christ, is a king, has a throne, and is victorious over the flesh, the world, and Satan.

3) Where is the millennium? It is on earth, but it is quite different from the earthly millennium of premillennialists.

4) What is meant by "judgment was given unto them"? The postmillennial explanation is that saints in different ways assist Christ as He judges and controls earthly affairs during their millennium or golden age. It has nothing to do with the final judgment where all will be judged by the one judge – Christ.

5) What is meant by "mark of the beast"? It is defined as figurative, not literal, language. All wicked people have certain marks of identification just as the Lord's people have marks or traits that identify them.

6) What is the duration of the millennium? Postmillennialists say it is not a literal thousand-year period, but is a figurative expression of a complete time period. They are not agreed upon when or if the millennium has begun.

7) What is meant by "rest of the dead"? It refers to all those physically living on the earth during the millennium who are spiritually dead. Only the born again (those resurrected to spiritual life) live with Christ. Others are

physically alive but spiritually dead and cannot reign with Christ.

8) What is meant by "first resurrection"? To postmillennialists it means those who are born again spiritually, those who are resurrected from a spiritually dead state (Jn. 3:3,5; Col. 2:12,13; Jn. 5:24,25; Eph. 2:1). Most appear to teach that this is the total meaning of the expression – first resurrection. A few, however, say it is the beginning of the first resurrection, but its culmination is when the soul is later raised or translated to Heaven.

9) What is meant by "second death"? Postmillennialists basically agree with the premillennial explanation which has already been given in this section.

10) What about the symbols used in describing the millennium? Postmillennialists see much more symbolism in Revelation 20:4-6 than premillennialists. They do not believe the "thrones" to be literal material thrones, nor do they think the millennium is limited to the martyrs, etc. of John's day. The "beast" is certainly not taken to be an animal; some think he represents pagan Rome and his "image" the Holy Roman Empire. The "mark" of the beast is not taken to mean a literal mark, and the expression "a thousand years" is believed to be a figure of speech. The "first resurrection" is the new birth, a spiritual resurrection.

To postmillennialists this is properly interpreting the Bible rather than spiritualizing its meaning away.

The Amillennial Response

1) When does the millennium take place? All amillennialists believe that it precedes the Second Coming of Christ rather than following it. Generally they believe it

happens simultaneously with the binding of Satan, but a few believe the two millenniums are not parallel. To the amillennialists the millennium of Revelation 20:4-6 is a present reality; it covers roughly the time period between the first and Second Coming of Christ. This, of course, is a contrast to the premillennial concept in that it is futurist and to the postmillennial concept in that it is not sure if the millennium has yet begun.

The amillennial view concerning the time of the millennium is the only view which fits the concept that Revelation must first be applied to the generation existing when it was written. Accordingly, that generation need not despair over those who were being persecuted unto death, for they were being translated into Heaven where the figurative millennium was already in progress.

2) Who is in the millennium? Amillennialists generally believe that all saints who have died are presently in the millennium but not necessarily that John's vision included them all. His vision of Revelation 20:4-6 concerned first and foremost the suffering Christians of his generation. As such the vision is limited to those beheaded or martyred and possibly a second larger group that included other sufferers who had refused to receive the mark of the beast. This does not exclude Christians who have lived and died since that time, but they are not actually portrayed in the vision.

3) Where is the millennium? Most amillennial writers say it is in Heaven; this sets them apart from the other eschatological views. Why do most amillennialists claim the millennium is in Heaven rather than on earth? First, we know from the passage itself that the millennium is wherever the "thrones" are, for it says, "And I saw thrones, and they

sat upon them." The word translated "throne," "thrones" or "seat" is used 47 times in the book of Revelation, and the thrones appear to be in Heaven in all but three places. The three exceptions are: Satan's throne or seat is referred to in 2:13, a dragon's throne or seat in 13:2, and the throne or seat of a beast in 16:10. Since the word in all other places refers to something in Heaven, it is not likely that John would depart from that concept in Revelation 20:4.

Second, we know that the millennium was where disembodied souls were, for we read, "And I saw the SOULS of them that were beheaded for the witness of Jesus." John saw souls, not bodies, because the passage declares that they had been beheaded, which means someone had cut their heads off. Rather than seeing bodies without heads being alive, he saw the souls of those who had been beheaded. How could John have stated what he meant more plainly? Souls go to be with the Lord at death, but bodies do not. Yet, both premillennialists and postmillennialists tell us that the word "souls" here refers to living people with bodies. This concept comes from their theories, not from the passage itself. It is true that the word here translated "souls" is in a few Biblical instances translated to mean living people, but that cannot be true in this passage. The word "people" here cannot be substituted for "souls" for then the passage would read, "And I saw the PEOPLE of them that were beheaded." The sentence then would not make sense.

When commenting on the word here translated "souls," George L. Murray affirmed:

The Greek word translated souls is *psueke*; and while used in one hundred and five places in the New Testament, there are only five places in which it can possibly have reference to the body, and some of the five are debatable.[2]

Third, we know that the millennium is where Jesus lives for the passage declares, "And they lived and reigned with Christ…." But where does Christ live? According to Revelation 5:7, He lives wherever the throne of God is, and that is in Heaven. Revelation 12:5 reveals the same truth. It appears, therefore, that the millennium of Rev. 20:4 is in Heaven.

Some amillennialists, including Augustine, do not limit Revelation 20:4-6 to a heavenly scene. These generally believe the reigning with Christ begins when one is regenerated. It, therefore, is believed to include the regenerated who have not died as well as those who have passed from physical life. It is true that all regenerated persons are spiritually resurrected at the time of their new birth. The question is, did John include the regenerated in his millennial vision? Some amillennialists do not think so.

4) What is meant by "judgment was given unto them"? Amillennialists agree that it does not refer to their being judged at a final judgment. Throughout Revelation Christ is pictured as reigning victoriously from Heaven. He is able to judge and defeat an earthly dragon, beast, and false prophet. Try to picture a heavenly scene where Christ and His martyrs reign over and judge the earthly creatures symbolized as a dragon, a beast, and a false prophet, etc. Any person who can visualize this probably has the message with which John was trying to comfort his generation. Of course, it is also a comfort to all other generations.

5) What is meant by "mark of the beast"? Amillennialists occasionally take this as a figure of speech. More often they believe it is literal history. John lived in a day when Roman emperors attempted to deify themselves. Domitian had statues of himself made and commanded that

his subjects bow before them. There arose an enforcement committee to see that people bowed before these statues thereby acknowledging that Domitian was divine. Those who obeyed received an official seal without which a person could neither buy nor sell. This is probably what John had in mind when he referred to some who refused to receive a mark upon their bodies.

6) What is the duration of the millennium? Amillennialists do not take the expression "a thousand years" literally. It is a figure of speech used for an indeterminate but complete time period. In Revelation 20 it covers the time period from the binding of Satan (20:2) until he is loosed (20:7). This roughly covers the time period between the first and Second Coming of Christ. The reasoning for this position need not be repeated here; it is found in the section under the Binding of Satan. There it applies to the binding, and here it refers to the millennium.

7) What is meant by "rest of the dead"? Amillennialists do not believe that this expression alludes to the bodily resurrection of the wicked dead as premillennialists do. They are not agreed, however, on what it does mean. Some think it simply refers to the body part of the dead in contrast to the soul which is alive in Heaven during the millennium. After the symbolic thousand years, the body will be raised on resurrection day. This will be true for both the righteous and the wicked.

Other amillennialists do not emphasize the concept of the body in contrast to the soul, but do believe the general resurrection is in the mind of the author.

Still other amillennialists think that the "rest of the dead" refers to the spiritually dead in contrast to the believing dead. These, therefore, do not see a bodily resurrection in this expression for anyone good or bad. The believing dead come alive during the millennium and share in it while the spiritually dead do not. These quickly point out that the word translated "until" does not imply that the spiritually dead will reign with Christ after the symbolic thousand years. The word "until" sometimes means "to the time that" and not beyond (see 1 Sam. 15:35; Isa. 22:14). The wicked, instead, will experience the second death or lake of fire forever (vv. 6, 10).

8) What is meant by "first resurrection"? Amillennialists believe that the "first resurrection" is spiritual, not literal, terminology. The expression alludes to a spiritual resurrection, not a bodily resurrection. The term "first" is used to set this "soul" resurrection apart from the bodily resurrection. The spiritual resurrection is first in order, place, time, and importance. It is superior to the bodily resurrection, for without it there is only a bodily resurrection to damnation. This first resurrection begins with the new birth and culminates in the soul being raised or translated to Heaven at death.

That the new birth is a type of resurrection is made clear in the Bible (Jn. 3:3,5; Col. 2:12,13; Jn. 5:24,25; Eph. 2:1). John, however, in his vision centers his thoughts primarily upon the culmination of this process. John was trying to distinguish between the regular bodily resurrection frequently referred to in the Scripture and the resurrection he was speaking of. Thus he called his spiritual resurrection the first resurrection. Later in the chapter he did refer to the bodily resurrection and to the destination of those involved in it.

9) What is meant by "second death"? Amillennialists interpret this the same way as all millennialists. It is, therefore, not necessary to explain it again. One can simply look back to the premillennial response to this question.

10) What about the symbols used in describing the millennium? The answers given to the previous questions show that amillennialists find more symbolism in this passage than premillennialists. They firmly believe, however, that this is the only accurate way to understand its message; they also resent being told that they are spiritualizing away the Bible.

First the Loosing then the Ultimate Overthrow of Satan

Rev. 20:7-10

And when the thousand years are expired, Satan shall be loosed out of his prison, And shall go out to deceive the nations which are in the four quarters of the earth, Gog and Magog, to gather them together to battle: the number of whom is as the sand of the sea. And they went up on the breadth of the earth, and compassed the camp of the saints about, and the beloved city: and fire came down from God out of heaven, and devoured them. And the devil that deceived them was cast into the lake of fire and brimstone, where the beast and the false prophet are, and shall be tormented day and night for ever and ever (Rev. 20:7-10).

Amillennialists and postmillennialists may not always interpret this passage identically, but in the interest of time, it is not felt necessary to split every theological hair. Both of these groups have minor variations of interpretation within their camps, but generally they see much symbolism in this passage while premillennialists see a literal city and a literal or physical battle. To conserve time a premillennial versus a non-premillennial view will be presented.

The Premillennial View

The thousand years of verse 7 are usually taken to be an exact period of one thousand years. Satan is loosed after or at the end of this period and quickly deceives the nations. The final battle, called Gog and Magog, takes place at Jerusalem. According to premillennial chronology, this will be after the thousand-year period, and therefore cannot be the same as the Battle of Armageddon (Rev. 16:16) or the battle described in Revelation 19. These both precede the thousand year period.

The Battle of Gog and Magog is pictured as a bloody battle between Christ and His forces on one side and enemies that surround Jerusalem on the other side. Premillennialists often name nations such as the Soviet Union which they believe will be involved. The forces of Christ, however, win the physical battle, and Satan is placed in the lake of fire for eternity.

The Non-Premillennial View

The non-premillennial view holds that the expression "the thousand years" is a symbolic rather than an exact time period. There is no disagreement with premillennialists concerning Satan being loosed just prior to the final battle and his doom. The nature of the battle, however, is a different story.

To non-premillennialists the Battle of Gog and Magog is not a bloody physical battle but a pictorial one. John borrows the expression from the Old Testament where the last great battle of that dispensation is brought to the attention of his readers. The Gog and Magog of Ezekiel refer to the terrible domination of Antiochus Epiphanes of Syria over Israel. What more fitting symbol could John have found to picture the close of the new dispensation?

Accordingly, the "saints" and the "beloved city" are believed to be symbolic. The "saints" represent the church and the "beloved city" the place where the church is located. The church, however, is actually located all over the world, not just in Jerusalem. The enemy is also pictured as worldwide, not simply regional in nature. The expression, "in the four quarters of the earth" (v.8) means worldwide.

What we have in this battle is a pictorial scene of the complete destruction of the forces of evil. It is not a long drawn out physical struggle to which Christ is subjected; that would be humiliating, and He will not come a second time to be humiliated. Christ is simply pictured in this passage as bringing fire down out of Heaven to devour the enemy (see 2 Thess. 1:7-10). The enemy should probably be thought of as more than people; the enemy includes secular humanism, atheism, infidelity, materialism, false religions, and sin in every form. After the Battle of Gog and Magog, sin, Satan, and all his helpers will cease bothering the human race. The battle is final, and the victory is complete.

The Judgment

Rev. 20:11-15

And I saw a great white throne, and him that sat on it, from whose face the earth and the heaven fled away; and there was found no place for them. And I saw the dead, small and great, stand before God; and the books were opened: and another book was opened, which is the book of life: and the dead were judged out of those things which were written in the books, according to their works. And the sea gave up the dead which were in it and death and hell delivered up the dead which were in them: and they were judged every man according to their works. And death and hell were cast into the lake of fire. This is the second death. And whosoever was not found written in the book of life was cast into the lake of fire (Rev. 20:11-15).

This is the fourth and final section of Revelation 20. The binding of Satan, the reign of saints, and the loosing and ultimate overthrow of Satan have been covered. These three events are followed by the judgment. It would be repetitious to repeat all the views concerning this Great White Throne Judgment since they are fully explained in the chapter on Prophecy and the Judgment. The reader may wish to read that chapter again. Sufficient proof was given in that chapter to conclude that the judgment of Revelation 20:11-15 is none other than the general judgment that is presented elsewhere throughout the Scriptures.

Chapter Summary

How shall we conclude our study of Revelation 20? The premillennial interpretation, rather than being a key to the understanding of prophecy, actually hinders any true prophetic understanding. It has been shown that the one passage that is supposed to fully support the premillennial view actually is silent about all its major tenants such as Jews, Palestine, temple, sacrifices, increased productivity, longevity, etc.

On the other hand, it has been shown that a more symbolic interpretation harmonizes with the rest of the Bible, the language and purpose of Revelation as a whole, and chapter 20 in particular. Once the symbolism is understood, there is no necessity to reinterpret the whole Bible. The one chapter which is said to clearly teach an exact one thousand year earthly and visible reign of Christ simply does not do so. If premillennialism cannot succeed in Revelation 20, it cannot scripturally prevail anywhere.

Chapter 11

Prophecy and the Future

The reader was promised in the preface to this book that a clear arrangement of God's plan for the future would be presented. It was also promised that this presentation would be without speculative theorization. Many writers seem to think those prophets who make the most dramatic claims are the ones who will get the most attention. This may or may not be true, but people should be interested in one thing – truth. Beware of doctrines established by modern prophets who claim special visions, anointing's, and revelations. When exposing such teachers, this writer feels similar to Murray who wrote:

It gives us no pleasure, but rather sorrow to make these observations; but we feel that a devotion to Christ and his truth must take precedence over our deference to our fellow man, however highly regarded by ourselves and others.[1]

The Negative

It seems appropriate to deal first with the negative. Much is being promised as prophetic truth which in reality has no Biblical foundation. Many prophetic promises presently proclaimed as future events were actually fulfilled long ago. Others will be fulfilled in the new Heaven and earth of the future rather than in a future millennium.

The following prophetic claims should not be anticipated as future events:

1) The kingdom of God should not be thought of as some future political, economic, earthly, or Jewish kingdom. This does not mean that there is no future aspect of the kingdom. The kingdom prophesied in the Old Testament was set up by Christ at His first advent. It is not to be anticipated as a future event because it was not postpone in the first place (see chapter 3).

2) The prophetic Temple of Ezekiel 40-48 is not something to be built in the future. Ezekiel's prophetic Temple became a reality in ages past. All the sacrifices described by Ezekiel would not presently fulfill any purpose; they were only a shadow of Christ, the only real and sufficient sacrifice (see chapter 3).

3) Israel is not a nation with a special prophetic future. This is not to say she does not have a future. Israel is like all other nations; God no longer has a chosen nation. Christians have replaced Israel, and they will forever remain God's chosen people. Christians, however, are not confined to race, color, or national boundary lines. The wall of partition between Jew and Gentile has been broken down (Eph. 2:14) and will never be rebuilt. Neither does God presently have a separate plan for Israel and the church. Israel's only hope is in the church which Christ purchased with His own blood (see chapter 4).

4) Daniel's 70th prophetic week should not be thought of as something future. The promise of a future seven-year tribulation period based upon Daniel's 70th prophetic week is an expectation without Biblical support. It became history in the distant past (see chapter 5).

5) A separate gospel called the "kingdom gospel" by which people are supposed to be saved during a future tribulation period should not be anticipated. There will never be but one gospel capable of saving people from their sins, and that is the gospel of Christ (Gal. 1:6-9). Any reinstatement of Judaism with its sacrificial system would be an affront to Jesus Christ, the only true atonement for sin (see chapter 3).

6) Multiple bodily resurrections scattered over more than a thousand years should not be expected. There will be only one bodily resurrection in the future, and it will include both the righteous and the unrighteous (see chapter 8).

7) There will not be a secret rapture in the future. First Thessalonians 4:13-17 does not teach a future secret rapture of the righteous accompanied by fantastic crashes and wrecks of all descriptions. Such crashes, believed to result from the rapture of Christian operators, are pure fantasy (see chapter 8).

8) Multiple judgments scattered over more than a thousand years should not be anticipated. There will be one general judgment in the future, and it will include both the lost and saved, righteous and unrighteous, or sheep and goats (see chapter 9).

9) Jesus should not be expected to come again three times (rapture, revelation, and for the destruction of the universe). Neither should He be expected to come again in three phases (one before tribulation, one after tribulation but before an earthly millennium, and one after the millennium to burn the world, etc.). Christ will come one more time, and that coming will have only one phase. Every eye will see

the Lord including the very people who crucified Him (Rev. 1:7).

10) People should not expect a future thousand-year earthly millennium during which Christ will reign over the world from Jerusalem. Judaism will never be reinstated by Christ; neither will Jews ever be elevated above the rest of humanity. Such expectations result from a misapplication of prophecy (see chapter 10).

11) People should not anticipate a chance to be saved after Jesus returns; the time of salvation will be over. The Bible declares, "…Behold, now is the accepted time; behold, now is the day of salvation" (2 Cor. 6:2).

Jesus did come to save during His first advent, but when He comes the second time it will be "In flaming fire taking vengeance on them that know not God, and that obey not the gospel of our Lord Jesus Christ" (2 Thess. 1:8). That no one can obtain salvation after Jesus comes to judge is clearly taught in many passages of Scripture (Acts 17:31; Rom. 2:5,6,16; 2 Tim.2:8; 2 Pet. 2:9; 3:7,9; Jude 6).

In addition to the many clear and plain passages are the parables which give no hint of people's ability to be saved after Jesus comes. Among these are the Parable of the Tares (Matt. 13:24-30, 37-43) and the Parable of the Dragnet (Matt. 13:47-50). Also in Matthew 25 Jesus gives a parable concerning ten virgins, five of which were wise and five foolish. In this parable the coming of Christ is likened unto a Jewish wedding during which the bridegroom comes at an hour when the foolish virgins are asleep. It is then declared:

…The bridegroom came; and they that were ready went in with him to the marriage; and the door was SHUT. Afterward came also the other virgins, saying, Lord, Lord, open to us. But he answered and said, Verily I say unto you, I know you not. Watch therefore, for ye know neither the day nor the hour wherein the Son of man cometh (Matt. 25:10-13).

Clearly, when the bridegroom came, the door of opportunity was shut; time for preparation had run out. It will be the same when Jesus, the bridegroom, comes for His bride – the church. Christ will then shut the door of salvation (Lk. 13:25-28).

It is a harmful doctrine which teaches a chance to be saved after Jesus comes. It holds out a false hope that may very well cost multitudes their eternal souls. Many may conclude that there is no urgency about getting right with God. They may reason that if Jesus comes before they make preparation, there will still be plenty of time to be saved during the so-called tribulation period. The millennium is also pictured as a time when all those born during it will have a chance to get saved. This premillennial doctrine is based upon a misunderstanding of a few apocalyptic Scriptures. Such an interpretation does great violence to the Bible as a whole and may cause lost people to put off salvation until it is too late. This doctrine of salvation after Jesus comes, that is, salvation during a tribulation period, should be avoided like a deadly plague.

Not only do dispensationalists offer a false hope of obtaining salvation after Jesus comes, but they also offer a false method of salvation. According to them the Holy Spirit leaves the world alongside the raptured saints. People should remember that it is only through the Holy Spirit that one is drawn to God. Without Him, man can neither be regenerated nor effectively witness for Christ. Yet, dispensationalists tell us that a Jewish remnant without the Holy Spirit is going to convert multitudes by means of a restored "gospel of the kingdom" rather than by the "gospel of grace." What this doctrine actually says is, that we do not need the Holy Spirit nor the gospel of the grace of Jesus Christ. A reinstated Judaism with its kingdom gospel is expected to be more potent than the work of Christ and the operation of the Holy Spirit. Readers, beware!

It should be clearly understood that the Bible teaches there will be no chance of obtaining salvation after Jesus comes. The probation of the human race will then be over, and everyone will receive his/her eternal reward, good or bad (Heaven or Hell). Salvation is an urgent matter that must be taken care of now. Rest assured that Satan is well-pleased with the doctrine of a chance to be saved after Jesus returns.

The Positive

Amillennialists are frequently accused of dealing largely with the negative while paying little attention to any clear exposition of what can be expected. There may be some truth in this; therefore, the positive will be carefully presented. A number of events, whether considered good or bad, have been foretold by Biblical writers.

1) An increase in apostasy will occur. This does not mean that the church will cease to bear witness to Christ, but it does mean the witness will not be all that it could have been. This increase in wickedness will appear gradually as the whole world is populated faster than Christian conversions occur. The apostasy will dramatically increase just prior to the return of Christ, a period when Satan will be loosed (Rev. 20:3,7-10).

Paul made it clear that increased sinfulness is to be expected. He said, "Let no man deceive you by any means:

for that day shall not come, except there come a falling away first…" (2 Thess. 2:3). There may be disagreements about the time when this prophecy began to be fulfilled, but the fact of the falling away is without question. It appears that this falling away has been in progress for many years but evidently will intensify in the end-time. The church seems to be in a process of thinking more and more like the world. Such a union can definitely lead to apostasy.

Paul on another occasion wrote:

Now the Spirit speaketh expressly, that in the latter times some shall depart from the faith, giving heed to seducing spirits, and doctrines of devils; Speaking lies in hypocrisy; having their conscience seared with a hot iron; Forbidding to marry, and commanding to abstain from meats… (1 Tim. 4:1-3).

This passage does not tell exactly how widespread the departure from the faith will be, but it definitely predicts a departure. This departure has no doubt already begun, but may yet increase in magnitude.

Again Paul says, "But evil men and seducers shall wax worse and worse, deceiving, and being deceived" (2 Tim. 3:13). Yes, an increase in apostasy and wickedness is in accord with the Biblical forecast. Unfortunately, it can be expected to proceed.

2) There will be continuous tribulation. It will even intensify near the end. Any idea of Christians not having to suffer because they have taken a stand for God is contrary to Biblical teachings. Jesus said, "…In the world ye shall have tribulation: but be of good cheer; I have overcome the world" (Jn. 16:33). Christians are not guaranteed an escape from tribulation; they are, however, promised victory in spite of it.

Again Paul says, "Yea, and all that will live godly in Christ Jesus shall suffer persecution" (2 Tim. 3:12). The teachings of Christ clash with the philosophy of the world; those who stand with God will continue to feel the opposition of the enemy. It always has been that way, and it always will be. It is generally believed that only one of the twelve apostles died a natural death; the others were all killed because of their Christian faith. Even John was banished to the Isle of Patmos. The time, manner, and place of his death are the subject of considerable discussion. Why, in the light of this, should a future generation of Christians be raptured out of persecution? Christ and all His followers had to face severe opposition. The truth is, the Bible does not support a pretribulation rapture theory. Such a theory results from poor Biblical interpretation.

Paul told his converts, "...We must through much tribulation enter into the kingdom of God" (Acts 14:22). People need to be taught reality in order to prepare them for the inevitable. Christians are not doing either Christ or His followers any favor when they exaggerate God's plans for the future. Too many people are being promised ease, health, wealth, and prosperity if they will only turn to the Lord. These people may become disillusioned with Christianity when such promises are not fulfilled. Beware of any such promises; the Christian life is not predicted to be a bed of roses. To live for Christ is to suffer with Christ. Yes, Paul plainly reminded his converts, "...When we were with you, we told you before that we should suffer tribulation; even as it came to pass, and ye know" (1 Thess. 3:4). This is the only type of message that prepares Christians for reality. Those who are not willing to pay a price do not have the spirit of Christ and need not join His people. They will not last long since they are totally unprepared for battle.

It has already been pointed out that evil will intensify near the end and need not be enlarged upon here except to say that when evil increases, additional persecution will follow. Persecution is a fact and should be expected.

3) Satan will be loosed in the end-time. Closely related to the anticipated increase in wickedness is the predicted loosing of Satan. John says, "And when the thousand years are expired, Satan shall be loosed out of his prison, And shall go out to deceive the nations which are in the four quarters of the earth…" (Rev. 20:7,8). For some reason, known only to God, Satan will be given more freedom just before Christ comes. With some nations now closing their doors to Christianity, one is made to wonder if mankind is entering Satan's "little season."

4) The intermediate state will continue until Jesus comes. By intermediate state is meant the state of the dead from their death to the resurrection of the body. It is also called the disembodied state. When Christians die, their bodies go to the grave, but their souls go to live with the Lord. This will continue to happen until death is destroyed. The intermediate state of existence is Biblically pictured as good but not complete. The soul will never be complete without a body; those presently disembodied are not, therefore, in their final state. The final state will come when the body is resurrected, changed, and adapted to eternity. At that time a New Heaven and earth will await the righteous (2 Pet. 3:12,13; Rev. 21:1).

That the righteous, however, continue to experience life before their resurrection is taught in several Scriptural passages. One Biblical writer stated:

Therefore we are always confident, knowing that, whilst we are at home in the body, we are absent from the Lord...We are confident, I say, and willing rather to be absent from the body, and to be present with the Lord (2 Cor. 5:6-8).

Life, therefore, does not stop with death; it continues in an alternate form. Accordingly, a Christian's true home is with the Lord rather than in a physical body. Presently, the Christian is somewhat like a pilgrim.

Paul on another occasion wrote:

For me to live is Christ, and to die is gain. But if I live in the flesh, this is the fruit of my labor; yet what I shall choose I wot not. For I am in a strait betwixt two, having a desire to depart, and to be with Christ; which is far better (Phil. 1:21-23).

Surely Paul was saying that if he died he would actually be better off because he would go immediately to be with the Lord. This would not be true if the soul remained unconscious throughout the church age and until the resurrection of the body.

John, when speaking of Christians who had died before he wrote the book of Revelation, said:

And when he had opened the fifth seal, I saw under the altar the SOULS of them that were slain for the word of God, and for the testimony which they held: And they cried with a loud voice, saying, How long, O Lord, holy and true, dost thou not judge and avenge our blood on them that dwell on the earth? And white robes were given unto every one of them; and it was said unto them, that they should rest yet for a little season, until their fellow servants also and their brethren, that should be killed as they were, should be fulfilled (Rev. 6:9-11).

It is clear that John was speaking of Christians who had been killed while on earth but who were then in Heaven in soul form. In soul form they were conscious and spoke of those still on the earth. They were told to rest (v.11) and let God in His own time deal with those remaining on earth. Yes, there is an intermediate state for the righteous who die. If Jesus tarries, many others can expect to enter into it.

The wicked dead also live in an intermediate state appropriate for them. The Bible, however, has less to say about the state of the wicked. They presently suffer, but they await the consummation of their damnation. Their bodies will also be resurrected, changed, and adapted to eternity. For those not saved, this final state will be experienced in a lake of fire. John describes in these words what will happen to the wicked after they are resurrected and judged; "and death and hell were cast into the LAKE of FIRE. This is the second death. And whosoever was not found written in the book of life was cast into the LAKE OF FIRE" (Rev. 20:14,15). This, of course, was revealed to John, but it has not yet taken place. The lost can expect it to happen; God's Word says so. That the wicked suffer, however, before their resurrection, judgment, etc. is also revealed in the story of the Rich Man and Lazarus (Lk. 16:19-31).

There is, therefore, a disembodied state for both the righteous and the unrighteous. It is an intermediate state appropriate to each one's standing with God. Neither the saved nor the lost, however, are in their final state; that state is future.

5) The Battle of God and Magog will be completed in the end-time. This battle is not simply the last physical battle as often pictured. Instead, it is a pictorial scene of the complete destruction of the forces of evil; it is spiritual in nature. The writer of Revelation 20:7-10 borrows the name for his pictorial battle from the Old Testament Book of Ezekiel. There, it was the last great battle of the old dispensation. It was a battle in which an evil prince – Antiochus Epiphanes – of Syria marshaled his forces against Israel. The evil prince was called Gog while his country was called the land of Magog.

John uses the same pictorial name to describe the final struggle of the New Testament dispensation. In the New Testament, Satan is the evil prince, and he will be destroyed by Christ at His coming. Magog in the New Testament is the whole world. Sin, its author, and all his helpers will come to their end at the conclusion of this New Testament Battle of Gog and Magog. The victory is pictured as absolute; righteousness will then reign forever. This battle may be the same as the Battle of Armageddon pictured in Revelation 16. The principle of parallelism found in Revelation should be remembered (see chapter 10).

6) Christ will return bodily to the earth. Several aspects of Christ's coming should be considered.

First, there is the FACT of His coming. Jesus sought to comfort His followers concerning His imminent death, resurrection, ascension etc. In doing so He informed them that when He went away He would then prepare a place for them. He then added, "And if I go and prepare a place for you, I will some again, and receive you unto myself; that where I am, there ye may be also" (Jn. 14:3). This is a clear promise from the divine Son of God who will not lie.

Christ's coming can be expected; it is as sure as if it were already history.

Many followers of Christ watched Him bodily ascend into the sky until finally they could no longer see Him. Then angels said to Christ's followers, "...Ye men of Galilee, why stand ye gazing up into heaven? this same Jesus, which is taken up from you into heaven shall so come in like manner as ye have seen him go into heaven" (Acts 1:11). They saw Jesus leave bodily, and He will return the same way. It is a Biblical promise that will happen.

Time will not be taken to quote the many other Scriptural passages that prove the fact of Christ's coming. A partial list of them, however, includes Matthew 26:64; Mark 14:62; Luke 12:40; John 21:22; Philippians 3:20; 1 Thessalonians 1:10; 3:13; 5:23; 2 Thessalonians 1:7,8; 1 Peter 1:13; and 2 Peter 3:8-13. Yes, Christ is coming; it is sure to happen, and this fact should not be questioned.

Second, the TIME of His coming is unknown. This is true in spite of constant claims to the contrary. Numerous examples could be given of those who have set various dates for the return of Christ, but their prophecies have invariably ended in failure. The date setters use various prophetic passages and sometimes connect them with the establishment of Israel in 1948. The truth is, any theological scheme is false that allows people to figure out the time of Christ's return. If the dispensational rapture scheme were true, everyone living near the Second Advent could figure out when Christ would return. How could they do this? Dispensationalists assure us that Daniel's seventieth prophetic week is still future and will last seven years. They further assure us that the appearing of Christ to rapture the saints will not be His Second Coming because He will not touch the earth at that time. His Second Coming thus follows immediately the so-called seven-year tribulation period. Accordingly, all people have to do to know when Jesus will come is to count seven years from the anticipated rapture and Christ must then appear. Readers, beware!

But what does the Bible say about the time of Christ's coming? It declares, "But of that day and that hour knoweth no man, no, not the angels which are in heaven, neither the Son, but the Father. Take ye heed, watch and pray: for ye know not when the time is" (Mk. 13:32,33). Again Jesus said, "Watch ye therefore: for ye know not when the master of the house cometh, at even, or at midnight, or at the cockcrowing, or in the morning: Lest coming suddenly he find you sleeping" (Mk. 13:35.36). It is amazing that any would claim knowledge superior to that of the angels and Christ. Modern prophets whose interpretation of prophecy allows them to figure out when Christ will return should be universally rejected.

Third, the Bible reveals the NATURE of Christ's coming. It will be visible to all humanity; the dispensational secret rapture concept is not Scriptural. Remember that people saw Jesus ascend visibly, personally, and bodily. As they watched, the angels said, "…This same Jesus, which is taken up from you into heaven, shall so come in like manner as ye have seen him go into heaven" (Acts 1:11). Also, John said, under divine inspiration, "Behold, he cometh with clouds; and EVERY EYE shall see him, and they also which pierced him; and all the kindreds of the earth shall wail because of him. Even so, Amen" (Rev. 1:7). Contrary to this plain statement, dispensationalists insist that only the righteous will see Him when He comes in the air. The Word of God declares that even those Jews and Romans who crucified the Lord will see Him. For further reference see also Mark 13:26 and 2 Thessalonians 1:7.

Not only will the Lord's coming be visible to all, but it will also be audible to all. Jesus said:

Marvel not at this: for the hour is coming, in which ALL that are in the graves shall hear his voice, And shall come forth; they that have done good, unto the resurrection of life; and they that have done evil, unto the resurrection of damnation (Jn. 5:28,29).

Yes, the voice of Jesus at His return will be audible enough to wake up all the dead. His so-called secret coming described in 1 Thessalonians sounds mighty noisy. There Paul says, "For the Lord himself shall descend from heaven with a shout, with the voice of the archangel, and with the trump of God..." (1 Thess. 4:16).

The Bible clearly teaches that when Jesus comes His body will be visible to all humanity and His voice will be heard by all. Humanity can anticipate it; it is a Biblical fact.

Fourth, the Bible reveals the PERSONALITIES involved in Christ's coming. First, angels will accompany and assist Christ at His coming.

For the Son of man shall come in the glory of his Father with his ANGELS...(Matt. 16:27).

When the Son of man shall come in his glory, and all the holy ANGELS with him, then shall he sit upon the throne of his glory (Matt. 25:31).

And to you who are troubled rest with us, when the Lord Jesus shall be revealed form heaven with his mighty ANGELS (2 Thess. 1:7).

These three verses are not the only Biblical passages which teach that angels will accompany Christ when He returns, but they should be sufficient to prove the point.

Not only will angels be with Christ, but the saints (Christians) in their disembodied or intermediate state will also come with Him. At the resurrection these disembodied saints will receive their eternal bodies; that is, bodies adapted to eternity. Jude spoke of these saints when he said, "… Behold, the Lord cometh with ten thousands of his SAINTS" (Jude 14). Of course "ten thousands" should be taken as a figure of speech; it represents all of God's saints.

Again the Bible declares, "For if we believe that Jesus died and rose again, even so them also which sleep in Jesus will God bring WITH him" (1 Thess. 4:14). No distinction should be made between Christ's coming WITH and FOR His saints. He will come both WITH and for them at the same time. He will come both WITH the disembodied saints and FOR those with earthly bodies. Both groups of saints will then receive a new body, hallelujah!

It is, therefore, maintained that two groups will accompany Christ when He returns – angels and the spirits of those who have died prior to His coming.

7) The bodies of Christians who have died will be resurrected. This will be first in the order of events when Christ comes. When speaking concerning this order of events, Paul said, "…And the dead in Christ shall rise first: Then we which are alive and remain shall be caught up together with them in the clouds to meet the Lord in the air…" (1 Thess. 4:16,17). The dead in Christ will be resurrected before the living Christians go anywhere. The dead will be raised first, and then they will go together to be

with the Lord. The wicked dead will be raised in the same hour (Jn. 5:28,29), but Paul makes the first order of events deal with the righteous.

8) Living Christians will be transformed. Christians who are living when Jesus returns will not need to be resurrected from the dead. Their bodies, however, will also have to be transformed and made ready for eternity. Paul affirmed:

Behold, I shew you a mystery; We shall not all sleep, but we shall all be changed, In a moment, in the twinkling of an eye, at the last trump: for the trumpet shall sound, and the dead shall be raised incorruptible, And we shall be changed (1 Cor. 15:51,52).

The souls of the righteous dead have already been redeemed, but the redemption of their bodies must wait until Christ comes again. When speaking concerning this, one Biblical writer said, "... Even we ourselves groan within ourselves, waiting for the adoption, to wit, the redemption of our body" (Rom. 8:23).

9) The wicked who are living will be burned along with the earth when Christ comes. It is a "tribulation" that the unsaved must suffer. When speaking to the righteous concerning the wicked who had greatly troubled them, Paul encouraged them by saying:

Seeing it is a righteous thing with God to recompense tribulation to them that trouble you; And to you who are troubled rest with us, when the Lord Jesus shall be revealed from heaven with his mighty angels, In flaming FIRE taking vengeance on them that know not God... (2 Thess. 1:6-8).

The coming of Christ is the great hope of Christians, but it will clearly be a time of destruction for all non-Christians.

10) The wicked dead will also be resurrected and transformed. While ALL the dead will be raised in the same hour (Jn. 5:28,29), the order is the righteous first and then the wicked. For the wicked there will be a resurrection to damnation (Jn. 5:29). It will occur after the righteous are raptured into the air; nevertheless, it will be in the same hour. Naturally, the bodies of those unsaved must be adapted to the eternal state else they would simply burn up. Neither the bodies of the righteous nor the unrighteous are presently ready for their state of eternal existence. A transformation must first occur; after that change there will be no more death.

11) All will be resurrected at the coming of Christ. This is true even though a moment of time may exist between the resurrection of the righteous and the wicked. Remember that Paul spoke of it all happening "In a moment, in the twinkling of an eye..." (1 Cor. 15:52). That is fast; God can complete the task as rapidly as one can blink his/her eye (see chapter 8).

12) All will be judged and properly rewarded at the coming of Christ (chapter 9).

13) Satan will someday be defeated and punished eternally. This is a Biblical promise. He has caused terrible problems for the human race, but his restricted freedom shall end. Satan will be completely and finally defeated by Christ at His coming. His sentence has already been pronounced, but when Christ comes, it will be executed. Just before the end Satan will be loosed, or restricted less, according to the writer of Revelation. He will go out to deceive all nations in the four quarters of the earth. Satan will obtain a great number of followers who will oppose all the children of God,

but then the mighty Christ will appear. Speaking of this time, John wrote:

…And fire came down from God out of heaven, and devoured them. And the devil that deceived them was cast into the lake of fire and brimstone, where the beast and the false prophet are, and shall be tormented day and night for ever and ever (Rev. 20:9,10).

This execution is a promise, and Satan is very much aware that it is going to happen (Rev. 12:12). No, Satan will not, as sometimes pictured, use a fork to turn the lost in the flames of Hell. His reign will end when Christ comes; he will literally be punished alongside those whom he deceived. Christian friends, Satan will then never again hurt you; he is the one who will be hurting.

14) The earth and universe are to be burned and then re-created. Speaking of the day when the Lord returns, Peter wrote:

But the day of the Lord will come as a thief in the night; in the which the heavens shall pass away with a great noise, and the elements shall melt with fervent heat, the earth also and the works that are therein shall be burned up. Seeing then that all these things shall be dissolved, what manner of persons ought ye to be in all holy conversation and godliness, Looking for and hasting unto the coming of the day of God, wherein the heavens being on fire shall be dissolved, and the elements shall melt with fervent heat? Nevertheless we, according to his promise, look for new heavens and a new earth, wherein dwelleth righteousness (2 Pet. 3:10-13).

The ungodly will be burned in this fire for Peter says, "But the heavens and the earth, which are now, by the same word are kept in store, reserved unto FIRE against the day of judgment and perdition of ungodly men" (2 Pet. 3:7).

Other Biblical writers also spoke of this destruction of the universe and the new creation which is to follow it (Job 14:12; Isa. 65:17; Matt. 24:35; Acts 3:21; Rom. 8:20-23; Rev. 20:11; 21:1). When the earth is created new it will no longer be necessary to pray that part of the Lord's Prayer which says, "thy kingdom come, Thy will be done in earth, as it is in heaven" (Matt. 6:10). It will then be a reality in the fullest sense of the word. Sin will no longer exist on the earth. Heaven and earth will become one. The earth will then be full of the knowledge of the Lord as waters now cover the sea (Isa. 11: 9; Hab. 2:14). Jesus will reign on the earth forever instead of for a thousand years.

15) Heaven and earth will be merged into one place, and the New Jerusalem will descend into it. When speaking of this future event, John said, "And I John saw the holy city, new Jerusalem, coming down from God out of heaven, prepared as a bride adorned for her husband" (Rev. 21:2). This is probably pictorial language that should not be over literalized. The New Jerusalem seems to be none other than the bride of Christ (Christians or saints) which will be above the earth while it is being burned and created new. Then Christ and His own will descend to the earth. Some new physical surroundings could possibly descend with them. This is when the marriage supper of the Lamb will occur. It will happen at the time of introduction to the eternal state. The wedding is only after the destination of all mankind has been determined. There is no Biblical support for a marriage supper at a pretribulation rapture. John puts the wedding in its rightful place not only in the first part of Revelation 21 but also later. John said an angel admonished him in these words:

...Come hither, I will shew thee the bride, the Lamb's wife. And he carried me away in the spirit to a great and high mountain, and shewed me that great city, the holy Jerusalem, descending out of heaven from God (Rev. 21:9,10).

John continues his picture of the future by saying, "And I heard a great voice out of heaven saying, Behold, the tabernacle of God is with men, and he will dwell with them, and they shall be his people, and God himself shall be with them, and be their God" (Rev. 21:3). Heaven will come down and merge with the new earth; they will become one. The earth will be greatly enlarged when Heaven descends and the sea is removed (Rev. 21:1). It will be something of a restored Garden of Eden except it will be universal.

16) Death will be destroyed before the righteous enter their ultimate inheritance. While continuing to describe the new Heaven and earth, John said, "And God shall wipe away all tears from their eyes; and there shall be no more DEATH, neither sorrow, nor crying, neither shall there be any more pain: for the former things are passed away" (Rev. 21:4). In the final state, there will not be any cancer, heart attacks, organ failures, painful divorces, etc. Such things cannot have any place in the final abode of the children of God.

Chapter Summary

Without undue speculation several promises have been established. There is yet to be an increase in apostasy. Christians are going to suffer continuous tribulations. Satan is to be loosed in the end-time. The intermediate state will continue until Jesus comes. The final struggle with Satan and his followers will end in a pictorial scene called the Battle of Gog and Magog.

The coming of Christ will be followed by a number of events. The bodies of Christians who have died will be resurrected and along with the bodies of living saints adapted to eternity. The living wicked will be burned to death and then all the wicked will be adapted to live in the lake of fire forever. All will be judged and properly rewarded. Satan, himself, will be defeated and cast into the lake of fire to suffer eternally. This earth and universe will be burned but replaced with a new Heaven and earth. The new Heaven and earth will be united and become one place. Death, and all sufferings associated with it, will be destroyed. Christ and His bride (Christians) will live together eternally in a perfect world, hallelujah!

Chapter 12

Prophecy Summarized and Concluded
The Importance of Eschatology

Some might say, "Why all the argument concerning dispensational premillennialism, historical premillennialism, postmillennialism, and amillennialism? They may further ask, "Why attach such importance to an issue that will not cause God to exclude any of His creation from their heavenly home?" It is a pleasure to answer these questions.

First, it is possible that ultra-dispensationalism will cause people to be excluded from Heaven. When anyone goes so far as to proclaim that the cross of Christ was not in God's plan, they are leaving out God's one and only plan of salvation. Christ can replace Judaism, but Judaism cannot replace Christ. Christ was the only real sacrifice; the animal sacrifices of Judaism were only a shadow or picture of the real. Furthermore, the dispensational doctrine which teaches that many will be saved during a future tribulation period by means of another gospel (kingdom gospel), rather than by the gospel of Christ, is a false plan of salvation. The Biblical response to such doctrine is that it is a perversion of truth which leads to condemnation (Gal. 1:6,9). Such doctrine may cause people to put off the only true gospel until it is too late; that is, until after Jesus comes.

Second, it is gladly acknowledged that in most cases one's eschatological position will not cause him/her to be excluded from Heaven. This does not mean, however, that what one believes is unimportant. Who wants his/her child to adopt the attitude that any behavior is acceptable as long as it is not serious enough for the parent to exclude him/her from the household? No parent would approve of such an attitude in his child. Why would anyone think that the heavenly Father would approve of such an attitude in His children? An issue does not have to be a life or death issue to be of value. Anything, which gets as much attention as eschatological matters in the Bible, must not be looked upon as unimportant. The Lutheran writer, Dr. A. L. Plueger warns:

...Bible believers in alarming numbers are being painted into a corner by a wrong understanding of prophecy. Experience shows that if things do not turn out as their teachers are saying, people will doubt the credibility of the Bible and some may forsake the faith.[1]

Those who look upon eschatology as nothing more than speculation concerning future events are wrong. Eschatology involves attitudes and relationships which are worldwide in scope. For example, groups who presently consider the Jews as God's chosen people may apply political pressures which will lead to another Arab and Israeli war. Such a war could conceivably be very broad in scope. Not only would such groups be guilty of causing war, but they would also be guilty of racism, and this is anti-biblical (Acts 10:34,35). Jews are not automatically right and Arabs wrong. Justice ought to be determined without respect of race. Christians are the only chosen people of God today, and every race has an equal opportunity in Christianity.

The Comparison of Millennial Views

Dispensational Premillennial View

The dispensational system is filled with serious errors. The author makes no apology for this stand; its advocates are the one who perpetuate such doctrines. In summary these errors include:

1) Their kingdom postponement theory.
2) Their theory that makes the cross unnecessary.
3) Their church parenthesis theory.
4) Their racist attitude.
5) Their method of Biblical interpretation which destroys the unity of the Scriptures.
6) Their concept that Israel and the church are two separate bodies of God with two separate purposes and destinies.
7) Their method of time calculation which allows people to know when Christ is coming.
8) Their secret rapture theory.
9) Their theory of a future tribulation period based upon Daniel's 70th prophetic week.
10) Their "gospel of the kingdom" theory.
11) Their concept that people can be saved after Jesus comes.
12) Their concept that people can be saved after Jesus comes by a kingdom gospel that is incapable of saving people.
13) Their theory of a future reinstatement of Judaism.
14) Their concept that the Holy Spirit will not be necessary to bring people to salvation when the kingdom gospel is reinstated.

15) Their theory of an earthly Jewish dominated millennium.

16) Their theory of multiple comings or phases to Christ's coming.

17) Their theory of multiple resurrections.

18) Their theory of multiple judgments.

While dispensationalism logically leads to an acceptance of all of the errors just listed, some who call themselves dispensationalists shy away from a few of the concepts.

Historical or Classical Premillennial View

Historical premillennialism is drastically different from its dispensational counterpart. Those holding to this view are able to avoid the more serious errors of dispensationalism. In fact, when one looks through the list of dispensational errors, he/she will find only a few with which historical premillennialists will agree. They do hold to more than one future resurrection and judgment but fewer in number than dispensationalists. Historical premill-ennialists also believe in a future earthly millennium, but not necessarily one in which Jews will be superior to Gentiles.

While this author differs with historical premillennialists on several issues, he sees them as being much more accurate in Biblical interpretation than dispensationalists. This writer would be pleased to see all people convert to amillennialism, but realistically does not expect that to happen. If historical premillennialists will not convert from the premillennial camp, it is honestly hoped that they will have success in taking back from dispensationalists that which dispensationalists earlier took from them. In early church history there was only one type of premillennialism and that was the historical variety. The world would be better off if this were true today.

Frankly, there is little evidence to make one believe non-dispensational premillennialists will regain control of premillennialism. Historical premillennialists have less zeal than their counterpart. They allow dispensationalists to speak for the whole of premillennialism. Sure, it is possible that the situation could change. Dispensationalism started with one person and in time found a way to dominate premillennialism. It is, therefore, not impossible to reverse the situation, but it will not be easy.

Postmillennial View

As far as eschatological beliefs are concerned, post-millennialists are correct most of the time. What they and amillennialists have in common far exceeds the few differences they have. Postmillennialists and amillennialists should think of themselves as allies with a common opponent – dispensationalism.

Postmillennialists hold that in the future the world is to become basically Christianized. Amillennialists disagree, and on this issue believe like the premillennialists who think evil will become even more widespread as time progresses. It is not a matter of one side believing the Bible, and the other rejecting it. It seems that the postmillennialists error in their interpretation of a few Biblical passages (Num. 14:21; Ps. 72; Isa. 2:2-4; 11:9; 35:1; 65:17-25; Jer. 31:34; Dan. 7:27; etc.).

Amillennialists also think postmillennialists are wrong on their view of both the nature and location of the millennium. Furthermore, Amillennialists reject the concept of a distant future return of Christ. It just does not seem to harmonize with the constant Biblical challenge to watch, be ready, etc.

We repeat, however, that in eschatology the postmillennialists are usually correct. They are to be commended for this. In fact, it will be great if their concept of world Christianization materializes.

Amillennial View

This author thinks amillennialism is the best of all eschatological views. The reasons for this high opinion of amillennialism have been fully explained throughout this book. Amillennialism, is not some "Johnny-come-lately" system of eschatology. It is as old as the Bible. Most of the church fathers, including Augustine, were amillennialists. Practically all of the reformers who brought about the Protestant Reformation were amillennialists. The list includes Calvin, Luther, Zwingli, Knox, and many others. Premillennialists frequently admit the fact that almost all of the reformers were amillennialists. The amillennialists of today can be grateful for their long and illustrious heritage and for doctrines that are Biblically sound. They remain the majority opinion among conservative scholars as a whole. Unfortunately, however, it is true that dispensationalism is the majority opinion among fundamentalists and it is growing rapidly.

Our ratings of the four major eschatological views from the worst (dispensationalism) to the best (amillennialism) does not, however, tell the whole story. When it comes to zeal and success, the dispensationalists are unsurpassed. This author is aware of the fact that a number of seasoned dispensationalists have left dispensationalism, but wholly disagrees with those writers who see dispensationalism as a dying breed. Dispensationalists can stand the losses because they are capturing and training an increasing percentage of youth. They are using television and the pen more successfully than any other eschatological group. In a relatively short span of time, dispensationalists have come from non-existence to dominance in some growing segments of Christianity. It is time for those of other eschatological views to recognize the magnitude of the task before them. Dispensationalism is so radical and potentially dangerous that there needs to be a united reaction against it.

Concluding Remarks

The stated purpose of this book was fourfold. First, it promised to expose serious errors in dispensationalism. Second, it promised by means of one volume to clarify the different views of eschatology. Third, it promised to establish from the Bible a clear arrangement of God's plan for the future without speculative theorization. Fourth, it promised to demonstrate the importance of eschatology itself. It does make a difference what one believes because beliefs are transformed into worldwide relationships. Neither present realities nor future expectations have been ignored. As a result, this writer believes all four commitments have been fulfilled.

Hopefully the pages of this book will contribute to a Biblical understanding that is pleasantly satisfying to its readers. May each reader be able to rest in peace concerning his/her particular eschatology. And may every reader, clergy and laity alike, be challenged to rise up and stand for the faith once delivered to the saints (Jude 3). No other faith or gospel can lead people to Heaven! The decision is yours. Please accept the challenge.

Notes:

Chapter 1

1- Walvoord, *Millennial Kingdom,* p. 231.

2- Ryrie, *Dispensationalism Today,* p. 146.

3- Pentecost, *Things to Come,* pp. 563-580.

4- Walvoord, *Millennial Kingdom,* p. 329.

5- Berkhof, *Systematic Theology,* p. 710.

6- Harrison, *The End,* p.111.

7- Buswell Jr., *A Systematic Theology of the Christian Religion,* vol. 2, pp. 393, 394.

8- Sharrit, *Soon Coming World-Shaking Events.*

9- Hoekema, *The Bible and the Future,* p. 136.

10- Adams, The Time Is at Hand, p.91.

Chapter 2

1- Cox, *The Millennium,* p. 22.

2- Hamilton, *The Basis of Millennial Faith,* p. 53.

Chapter 3

1- DeHaan, *The Second Coming of Jesus,* p. 98.

2- Blackstone, *Jesus is Coming,* p. 84.

3- *Ibid,* p. 88.

4- Lindsey, *There's a New World Coming*, p. 30.

5- Gordon, *Quiet Talks About Jesus*, p. 114.

6- Boettner, *The Millennium, revised edition*, p. 223.

7- Lindsey, *There's a New World Coming*, p. 30.

8- Larkin, *Rightly Dividing the Word*, p. 53.

9- Ford, *Seven Simple Sermons on the Second Coming*, p. 48.

10- Hughes, *A New Heaven and a New Earth*, p. 160.

11- North, *Armageddon When? A Reply to Hal Lindsey*, p. 17.

Chapter 4

1- Chafer, *Dispensationalism*, p. 448.

2- Ryrie, *The Basis of the Premillennial Faith*, p. 12.

3- Walvoord, *Millennial Kingdom*, pp. vii, viii.

4- Hoekema, *The Bible and the Future*, p. 198.

5- Hendriksen, *Israel in Prophecy*, pp.56, 57.

6- Chafer, *Dispensationalism*, pp. 40, 41.

7- Chafer, *The Kingdom in History and Prophecy*, p. 70.

8- Gordon, *Quiet Talks About Jesus*, p. 114.

9- *Ibid*, p. 118.

10- Boettner, *The Millennium*, p. 220.

11- Murray, *Millennial Studies*, p. 57.

Chapter 5

1- *Ibid*, p. 98.

2- John L. Bray, *The Great Tribulation*, p. 12.

3- Jones, *The Great Tribulation*, p. 58.

4- Iornside, *The Great Parenthesis*, p. 50.

Chapter 6

1- Boettner, *The Millennium*, p. 210.

Chapter 7

1- Jones, *The Great Tribulation*, p. 72.

2- Cox, *Biblical Studies in Final Things,* p. 103.

3- Hoekema, *The Bible and the Future*, p. 130.

4- Larkin, *The Book of Revelations,* pp. 26, 27.

5- *Ibid*, p. 67.

Chapter 8

1- Carver, *When Jesus Comes Again*, p. 319.

2- Chafer, *Systematic Theology*, vol 4, p. 400.

Chapter 9

1- Boettner, *The Millennium*, p. 276.

2- Dunham, ed., *Unvieling the Future*, p. 60.

3- Chafer, *Systematic Theology*, vol. 4, p. 406.

4- *Ibid*, p. 411.

5- *Ibid*, p. 412.

Chapter 10

1- Boettner, *The Millennium*, p. 127.

2- Murray, *Millennial Studies*, p. 183.

Chapter 11

1- *Ibid*, p. 71.

Chapter 12

1- Pleuger, *Things to Come for Planet Earth*, p. 6.

Bibliography

Amillennialism

Adams, Jay. *The Time Is at Hand. Phillipsburg*, N.J.: Presbyterian and Reformed Pub. Co., 1966.

Allis, Oswald T. *Prophecy and the Church*. Phillipsburg, N.J.
 Presbyterian and Reformed Pub. Co., 1945.

Berkhof, Louis. *Systematic Theology*. Grand Rapids, Mich.:
 Eerdmans, 1941.

--, *The Second Coming of Christ*. Grand Rapids, Mich.: Eerdmans,
 1953.

Berkouwer, G. C. *The Return of Christ*. Grand Rapids, Mich.:
 Eerdmans, 1972.

Bray, John. L. *The Battle of Gog and Magog.* Lakeland, Fla.: John L.
 Bray Ministry, Inc., 1987.

--. *The Coming of Christ in First and Second Thessalonians.* Lakeland,
 Fla.: John L. Bray Ministry, Inc., 1987.

--. *The Great Tribulation*. Lakeland, Fla.: John L. Bray Ministry, Inc.,
 1987.

--. *Israel in Bible Prophecy*. Lakeland, Fla.: John L. Bray Ministry,
    Inc., 1983.

--. *A Look at the book of Revelation,* Lakeland, Fla.: John L. Bray
    Ministry Inc., 1984.

--. *The Millennium – The Big Question*, Lakeland, Fla.: John L. Bray
    Ministry Inc., 1984.

--. *The Origin of the Pre-Tribulation Rapture Teaching.* Lakeland,
    Fla.: John L. Bray Ministry, Inc., 1982.

--. *The Second Coming of Christ*, Lakeland, Fla.: John L. Bray
    Ministry, Inc., 1985.

Carver, Everett I. *When Jesus Comes Again.* Phillipsburg, N.J.:
    Presbyterian and Reformed Pub. Co., 1979.

Cox, William E. *Amillennialism Today.* Phillipsburg, N.J.:
    Presbyterian and Reformed Pub. Co., 1966.

--. *Biblical Studies in Final Things.* Phillipsburg, N.J.: Presbyterian and
    Reformed Pub. Co., 1980.

--. *An Examination of Dispensationalism.* Phillipsburg N.J.:
    Presbyterian and Reformed Pub. Co., 1980.

--. *The Millennium.* Phillipsburg, N.J.: Presbyterian and Reformed
    Pub. Co., 1964.

--. *The New-Covenant Israel.* Phillipsburg, N.J.: Presbyterian and
    Reformed Pub. Co., 1962.

--. *Why I left Scofieldism.* Phillipsburg, N.J.: Presbyterian and
    Reformed Pub. Co., 1978.

Currell, R. G. and Hurlbut, E. P. *The Ruler of the Kings on the Earth.*
    Phillipsburg, N.J.: Presbyterian and Reformed Pub. Co.,
    1982.

Hamilton, Floyd E. *The Basis of Millennial Faith.* Grand Rapids,
    Mich.: Eerdmans, 1942.

Hendriksen, William. *Israel in Prophecy.* Grand Rapids, Mich.: Baker,
    1968.

Hoekema, Anthony A. *The Bible and the Future.* Grand Rapids, Mich.:
    Eerdmans, 1979.

Hughes, Archibald. *A New Heaven and a New Earth.* Phillipsburg,
    N.J.: Presbyterian and Reformed Pub. Co., 1958.

Jones, R. Bradley. *The Great Tribulation.*
    Grand Rapids, Mich.: Baker,   1980.

--. *What, Where, and When Is the Millennium?* Grand Rapids, Mich.:
Baker, 1975.

Lewis, Arthur H. *The Dark Side of the Millennium.* Grand Rapids,
Mich.: Baker, 1980.

Mauro, Phillip. *The Gospel of the Kingdom.* London, England:
Hamilton Brothers, 1928.

--. The Seventy Weeks and the Great Tribulation. Swengel, Penn.: Bible Truth Depot, 1944.

Murray, George L. *Millennial Studies.* Grand Rapids, Mich.: Baker,
1960.

Nielson, Lewis. *Waiting for His Coming.* Cherry Hill, N.J.: Mack
Publishing Co., 1975.

Pieters, Albertus. *The Seed of Abraham.* Grand Rapids, Mich.:
Eerdmans, 1950.

--. *Studies in Revelation of St. John.* Grand Rapids, Mich.: Zondervan,
1937.

Plueger, Aaron Luther. *Things to Come for Planet Earth.*
St. Louis, Mo.: Concordia Publishing House, 1977.

Summers, Ray. *The Life Beyond*. Nashville, Tenn.: Broadman Press, 1959.

Travis, Stephen. *I Believe in the Second Coming of Jesus*. Grand Rapids Mich.: Eerdmans, 1982.

Vos, Geerhardus. *The Kingdom of God and the Church*. Phillipsburg, N.J.: Presbyterian and Reformed Pub. Co., 1972.

--. *The Pauline Eschatology. Grand Rapids,* Mich.: Eerdmans, 1930.

Wyngaarden, Martian J. *The Future of the Kingdom*. Grand Rapids, Mich.: Baker, 1955.

Young, Edward J. *The Prophecy of Daniel*. Grand Rapids, Mich.: Eerdmans, 1949.

Zens, Jon. *Dispensationalism.* Phillipsburg, N.J.: Presbyterian and Reformed Pub. Co., 1980.

Postmillennialism

Boettner, Loraine. *The Millennium. Phillipsburg*, N.J.: Presbyterian and Reformed Pub. Co., revised edition, 1984.

Campbell, Roderick. *Israel and the New Covenant*. Phillipsburg, N.J.: Presbyterian and reformed Pub. Co., 1954.

Hodge, Charles. *Systematic Theology*. New York, N.Y.: Charles Scribner and Co., 1872.

Kik, J. Marcellus. *An Eschatology of Victory*. Phillipsburg, N.J.:
Presbyterian and Reformed Pub. Co., 1971.

--. *Revelation Twenty*. Phillipsburg, N.J.:
Presbyterian Reformed Pub. Co., 1955.

Kimball, William R. *The Rapture: A Question of Timing.*
Grand   Rapids, Mich.: Baker, 1985.

King, Max R. *The Spirit of Prophecy*.
Warren, Ohio: Parkman Road
Church of Christ and Warren Printing Inc., 1971.

North, Stafford. *Armageddon When? A Reply to Hal Lindsey.*
Oklahoma City, Okla.: Oklahoma Christian College, 1982.

Strong, Augustus H. *Systematic Theology.*
Philadelphia, Penn.: Griffith and Roland Press, 1907.

Terry, Milton S. *Biblical Hermeneutics*.
Grand Rapids, Mich.: Zondervan, n.d.

Warfield, B. B. *Biblical Doctrines.* New York, N.Y.:
Oxford University Press. 1929.

Woodrow, Ralph. *Great Prophecies of the Bible.*
Riverside, Calif.:
Ralph Woodrow Evangelistic Association, Inc., 1971.

--. *His Truth Is Marching On*. Riverside, Calif.:
Ralph Woodrow Evangelistic Association, Inc., 1977.

Historical Premillennialism

Erikson, Millard J. *Contemporary Options in Eschatology.*
Grand Rapids, Mich.: Baker, 1977.

Hubbard, David Allen. *The Second Coming: What Will
Happen When Jesus Returns?*
Downers Grove, Ill.: Inter Varsity Press, 1984.

Ladd, George Eldon. *The Blessed Hope.*
Grand Rapids, Mich.: Eerdmans, 1956.

--. *Crucial Questions About the Kingdom of God.*
Grand Rapids, Mich.: Eerdmans, 1952.

Reese, Alexander. *The Approaching Advent of Christ.*
London, England: Marshall, Morgan, and Scott, 1937.

Rose, George L. *Tribulation Till Translation.*
Glendale, Calif.: Rose Pub. Co., 1943.

Dispensational Premillennialism

Blackstone, W. E. *Jesus Is Coming.*
New York N.Y.:   Revell, 1898.

Chafer, Lewis Sperry. *Dispensationalism.*
Dallas, Tex.: Dallas Seminary Press, 1951.

--. *The Kingdom in History and Prophecy.*
Chicago, Ill.:   Revell, 1915.

--. *Systematic Theology.*
Dallas, Tex.: Dallas Seminary Press, 1948.
Vol. 4 is eschatology.

Darby, John N. *Synopsis of the Books of the Bible*.
New York, N.Y.: Loizeaux Brothers, 1950.

DeHaan, M. R. *The Second Coming of Jesus*.
Grand Rapids, Mich.: Zondervan, 1978.

Dunham, T. Richard (Edited). *Unveiling the Future*.
Findlay, Ohio: Fundamental Truth Publishers, 1934.

Ford, W. Hershel. *Seven Simple Sermon on the Second Coming*.
Grand Rapids, Mich.: Zondervan, 1945.

Gaebelein, A. C. *The Prophet Daniel*. Grand Rapids, Mich.:
Kregel
Publications, n.d.

Gordan, S.D. *Quiet Talks About Jesus*.
Chicago, Ill.: Revell, 1906.

Hoyt, Herman A. *The End Times*.
Chicago, Ill.: Moody Press, 1969.

Ironside, H. A. *The Great Parenthesis*.
Grand Rapids, Mich.: Zondervan, 1943.

--. *The Lamp of Prophecy*.
Grand Rapids, Mich.: Zondervan, 1940.

Larkin, Clarence. *The Book of Revelation*.
Philadelphia, Penn.: Erwin W. Moyer Company Printers,
1919.

--. *Rightly Dividing the Word*. Philadelphia, Penn.:
Erwin W. Moyer Company Printers, 1921.

Lindsey, Hal. *The 1980's Countdown to Armageddon.*
King of Prussia, Penn.: Westgate Press, 1980.

--. *The Late Great Planet Earth.*
Grand Rapids, Mich.: Zondervan, 1970.

--. *There's a New World Coming.*
Ventura, Calif.: Vision House Publishers, 1973.

Pentecost, J. Dwight. *Prophecy for Today.*
Grand Rapids, Mich.: Zondervan, 1961.

--. *Things to Come.*
Findlay, Ohio: Dunham Pub. Co., 1958.
Grand Rapids, Mich.: Zondervan, 1958 rpt.

Ryrie, Charles C. *The Basis of the Premillennial Faith.*
Neptune, N.J.: Loizeaux Brothers, Inc., 1953.

--. *Dispensationalism Today.*
Chicago, Ill.: Moody Press, 1965.

--. *The Final Countdown,*
Wheaton, Ill.: Victor Books of SP Publications,Inc.,
1982.

Scofield, C. I. *The Scofield Reference Bible.*
London, England: Oxford Press, 1917.

Walvoord, John F. *The Millennial Kingdom.*
Findlay, Ohio: Dunham Pub. C., 1959.

Multiple Millennial Views

Clouse, Robert G. (Edited). *The Meaning of the Millennium: Four Views.* – George E. Ladd (Historical Premillennialism), Hermon A. Hoyt (Dispensational Premillennialism), Loraine Boettner (Postmillennialism), and Anthony A. Hoekema (Amillennialism).
Downers Grove, Ill.: Inter Varsity Press, 1977.

Ludwigson, Raymond. *A Survey of Bible Prophecy.*
Grand Rapids, Mich.: Zondervan, 1973.

Multiple Premillennial Views

Archer, Feinberg, Moo, and Reiter. *The Rapture: Pre-, Mid-, or Posttribulation?*
Grand Rapids, Mich.: Zondervan, 1984.

Pre Three and one Half Year Tribulation Premillennialism

Harrison, Norman B. *The End: Re-Thinking the Revelation.*
Minneapolis, Minn.: Harrison Service, 1941.

Mid-Tribulation Premillennialism

Buswell Jr., James O. *A Systematic Theology of the Christian Religion.*
Grand Rapids, Mich.: Zondervan, 1962.

Post Three and one Half Year Tribulation Premillennialism

Sharrit, John T. *Soon Coming World Shaking Events*. LaVerne, Calif.: El Camino Press, 1978.

Non-Dispensational Commentaries

Barnes, Albert. *Barnes' Notes.*
Grand Rapids, Mich.: Baker, 1961 rpt.

Clarke, Adam. Clarke's Commentary.
New York, N.Y.: Abingdon-   Cokesbury Press, n.d.

Davidson F. (Editor). *The New Bible Commentary*.
Grand Rapids, Mich.: Baker, 1953.

Hailey, Homer. *Revelation: An Introduction and Commentary*.
Grand Rapids, Mich.: Baker, 1979.

Hendriksen, William. *More Than Conquerors: An Interpretation of the Book of Revelation*.
Grand Rapids, Mich.: Baker, 1939.

Henry, Matthew. *Matthew Henry's Commentary*.
New York, N.Y.:   Revell, n.d.

Jernigan, Wade T. *The Unsealed Book: An Amillennial View of Revelation.*
Nashville, Tenn.:
Randall House Publications, 1975.

Summers, Ray. *Worthy Is the Lamb: An Interpretation of Revelation.*
Nashville, Tenn.: Broadman Press, 1951.

Index of Authors

Manufactured by Amazon.ca
Bolton, ON

13712137R00151